REFUSE
TO BE COMMON

TITUS CHU

Refuse to Be Common
by Titus Chu

May 2022

Distributed by
The Church in Cleveland Literature Service
3152 Warren Road
Cleveland, Ohio 44111

Available for purchase on Amazon.com
and asweetsavor.org.

Please send correspondence by email to
questions@asweetsavor.org

Published by
Good Land Publishers
Ann Arbor, Michigan

We proclaim Him, admonishing every man and teaching every man with all wisdom, so that we may present every man complete in Christ.
—Colossians 1:28

ENGLISH EDITOR'S FOREWORD—

A FRAGRANCE SWEET AND RARE

Margaret Emma Barber (1866–1930) was a rare sort of missionary. She served as she felt led by the Lord with little outward acknowledgment or signs of success. By the time she passed away in 1930, she had labored for decades in a small village with few possessions, no publications, and a small band of workers under her care. But by the end of those years, the Lord had raised up a generation of leaders through her. She poured herself into Watchman Nee, Faithful Luke, Leland Wang and dozens of others. While she was never widely known, these leaders shaped the landscape of Christianity in China and around the world for the rest of the century.

I have always enjoyed and been impressed by Miss Barber's hymn, "Thou Magnet of My Soul." In this hymn, she wrote a verse:

Thou Sunshine of my heart!
Fill Thou each crevice there,
And let Thy garden yield to Thee
A fragrance sweet and rare.

Miss Barber was not interested in the outward acknowledgement of others. She only desired that the garden of her life would bring a fragrance to the Lord that was uncommon—one that was "sweet and rare."

This effort to gain what is "sweet and rare" to the Lord is the heart of this book by Titus Chu. I was happy to hear it had been published in Chinese, then thrilled to hear it had been translated into English. In 2018, I personally attended the meetings in which brother Titus delivered these messages in English. I then heard that the content was delivered and even more well received when he gave the same messages in China later that year. I was eager to see how the material from both languages was put together to create this book.

Initially, I was quite disappointed.

When brother Titus ministers, his speaking flows. The content of this book, however, seemed choppy and his flow was hard to sense. More than that, the order of chapters was different from the order of the messages I heard in English. In English, brother Titus presented the material sequentially through the twenty points found in the Introduction. This book, however, follows more closely the ten bullet points found at the end of the Introduction, perhaps reflecting brother Titus's sharing in China. To add to my confusion, I discovered content marked in gray boxes throughout the book. Why did these boxes exist?[1] At times, this book almost felt like a collection of proverbs.

---

1 For the reader: because this book combined messages from two languages, some content could not be combined easily in the chapters. The gray boxes allow such content to be kept with the material it was originally connected to.

And yet...

I was affected.

As I spent time in this material and considered the statements made, I noticed my prayers being adjusted. I no longer merely asked for things from the Lord, but I began to seek His face apart from these things, to simply spend time in His presence, to ask Him that I could be more one with Him, and especially to ask that I could be an uncommon lover of Jesus—to develop, as Miss Barber writes, that "fragrance sweet and rare."

Dear reader, let me ask you, what is better?

A book that is smooth, that is enjoyable to read, that flows well, and then is set down and forgotten? Or,

A book that will affect you?

This book should and can affect us if we do not just look for an enjoyable time, but are open to the warnings within.

The Chinese editor notes that this is not a happy book. I agree; it is a book about what can go wrong in your Christian life—it is not happy! It will not pacify your conscience! But it does carry a fragrance "sweet and rare." May it produce a yearning within all readers to develop such a fragrance unto the Lord Himself.

Mark Miller
April, 2022

CHINESE EDITOR'S FOREWORD—

TO THE SIDE WAYS: "NO!"

In the North, snow falls quietly. Hardly a sound is heard, yet after one night, the snow can accumulate many feet, and the world is transformed to a white landscape. Indeed, in this whole process, there is no sound in the descending snowflakes and the accumulating snow.

The change comes silently, quietly, gradually. Few notice it at all, until we wake up in the morning to a changed world.

Oh, it is the unnoticable, quiet things that make walking the heavenly way so difficult! Unconsciously, we can drift from ascending to descending, from advancing to going backwards, from being spiritual to being fleshly, from being blessed to losing the blessing, and from the way of the Lord to a "side way," a broken and ruined stray path. At our weakest moments, we must be woken up by the night watchmen who are urgently sounding the warning alarm. Oh, saints, we must be awakened again and again!

The apostle Paul preached Christ and served the saints by warning every man and teaching every man in all wisdom, that he might present every man perfect in Christ Jesus (Col. 1:28). His warnings and teachings were like the soundings of the night alarms, issuing deep warnings to those who are pursuing the Lord's heavenly way.

In the same spirit, this book, *Refuse to Be Common,* is a book of warning.

It begins with both a question and its answer—

The question is:
Why can't many Jesus-lovers develop healthily all the way?

The answer is:
It is because they have unconsciously become common.

For various reasons outlined in this book, many Jesus-lovers go a side way without knowing it, and every side way leads them to become common.

It is for these many reasons that we need "warning signs" along the heavenly way. This book is a collection of these warning signs, signaling, "Caution, caution!" as each side way approaches. Becoming common may not seem drastic to the reader, but it is like a snare waiting to collect Jesus-lovers, to subdue them, to devastate them, and to rob away their development.

Based on his learning from the Bible, his experiences of following the Lord, and his serving of the church for many decades, the author of this book has positively seen a heavenly picture of growth in the Lord's divine life. Yet he has also noticed many dangers and side ways which may not be noticeable to others. In his eyes, the way of growth is a narrow way (see Matt. 7:13–14). Because it is narrow, few can find it and walk on it. It is like a narrow path through rocky cliffs, or like a tightrope hanging in the air. To remain on it requires careful vigilance with fear and trembling.

More precisely, this narrow way, the heavenly way, is the true way of the cross.

Though this book offers warning signs, only the cross can correct and direct the way. Only the death and resurrection that subjectively proceeds from the cross can keep and supply those who walk on this way.

This book is based on the messages of Brother Titus Chu in 2018, spoken in the United States and in China. He desires all Jesus-lovers to develop healthily, and in order to develop, we need to fight against being common! **Oh, reader, refuse to be common and refuse to walk on the side ways!** When Nehemiah rebuilt the wall of Jerusalem, the workers built with one hand and held a weapon with the other (Neh. 4:17). Today we are, on the one hand, walking positively on the heavenly way and, on the other hand, guarding against failure with the refusal to be common in the truth of the cross.

May the Lord gain those who are not common.

This book is dedicated to all who serve the Lord and desire the way of the Lord. Amen!

TABLE OF CONTENTS

PART 2 | Turning to a Sideway because of Ourselves

WORDS OF A WATCHMAN II

PART 3 | Turning to a Sideway Because of Our Condition with the Lord

INTRODUCTION—

A BOOK OF WARNING

Every Jesus-lover wants to serve the Lord full-time. Everyone who consecrates themself to the Lord wants to be His servant. Their life is a life of fighting—fighting against commonality, **refusing to be common.**

To be common is constituted in us. This is why the church life can so easily become a social life to many saints. Zealous brothers become cool; good brothers become indifferent. Why? It is because they don't realize that what they are doing makes them common. Oh, it is hard for us to realize how serious, yet how subtle, this matter is! Even those who are "successful" can rest in their attainment and become common. For example, preaching can easily make a brother common. For most preachers, if they are not simply enjoying their own speaking, then they are seeking for others' praises concerning their speaking. Both of these ways lead them to become common.

Brothers and sisters, as Jesus lovers, you need to learn to fight against commonality lifelong. Other people graduate from college in four years, but you may graduate in five years because you spent one year to pursue the Lord. This is not common. Other people seek a teaching job after getting a

PhD degree. This is actually very common. But if a brother is following the Lord absolutely, he can refuse to be common like the others.

On the earth today, many love the Lord, but there is no real consecration. Among those who consecrate to the Lord, there is no real development. What is the reason Jesus lovers cannot develop healthily? The reason is that they don't refuse to be common. It is too easy for us to love the Lord and even to say, "Lord, I give my life to You," but it is hard to develop healthily all the way to the end. This is because we become common.

Brothers,
The first stand you must make in your life is:

"I refuse to be common in my life!"

In other words, "I refuse to just have my choice. I refuse to just live by what I think is right. I refuse to just do what others do." Instead, desire to develop healthily all the way to the end. If this is not the case, what will be the lasting value of your loving the Lord and following the Lord? After graduation, worldly people look for a job and you also look for a job. Worldly people teach, and you also teach. Worldly people make money, and you also make money. Where is the value in that?

Twenty Sideways Paths; Twenty Warnings

All your life, you need to fight against being common! If you become common, you will not reach the Lord's desire for you. Brothers, I have seen this repeated again and again. Many love the Lord and follow the Lord in the beginning, but they become common and cannot develop healthily all the way. They depart sideways from the Lord's way for different reasons:

1. Change of environment
2. Marriage
3. Jobs/Professions
4. Disposition
5. Lacking a stern face—not focused on Christ alone in whatever the decisions we make
6. Different reasons of human relationships
7. Seeking attainment other than Christ, both in the Lord's work or human success
8. Getting settled easily
9. Independency—without protection, without companionship
10. Lacking a laboring field
11. Being possessed by a laboring field. The field replaces Christ.
12. Having self-pity in the existence of being a Jesus lover or in attainment, replacing purity in Christ
13. Also, having self-pity when passing through the Lord's governmental working
14. Zealous pursuing replacing proper laboring
15. Zealous laboring replacing a pure love and consecration to Jesus
16. Not knowing how to keep oneself low—overly trying to be appreciated, manifested, or in leadership

17. Taking advantage of the Lord's work, even of congregations, grasping whatever opportunity one may have in serving

18. One's outward operation developing more than one's inner life.

19. Becoming obsessed by spiritual things, rather than Christ, especially by preaching or being manifested in leadership

20. The focus given by the Lord can be deviated or distracted by a good living, the world, a healthy fresh burden and commitment, success of life, or success in serving the Lord.

These twenty points are twenty side paths, all leading to spiritual death. Brothers, these twenty points will not help you develop a rich ministry as you follow the Lord. However, if you can heed these twenty points, you may have a healthy spiritual life. You will be preserved. Take these twenty points as twenty warnings. When you are young in age, you can die spiritually and return to the Lord by repenting. But if you die spiritually at or over the age of forty, you will lose your usefulness to the Lord. The way you love the Lord at that age will ruin you, because you have actually become quite common, but it is hard for you to change.

Being Common because of Ourselves and because of Our Condition with the Lord

Please note that these twenty warnings are twenty definite turnoffs from the Lord's path for us. They are a result of ten principles that operate to make us common. These ten principles can be divided into two groups. Some of these principles are sideways paths themselves, while other principles produce multiple sideways paths. The first group is a collection of sideways that come from ourselves. The second group is a collection of sideways that come because of our condition with the Lord.

In the first group are five general principles:

- The lack of a stern face facing Jerusalem
- The lack of the being and the constitution of acacia wood
- Being self-centered
- Not respecting marriage
- Overly focusing on personal development

In the second group, there are also five general principles:

- Easily settling down
- "Elevating" ourselves by what we have
- Zealous pursuing replacing proper laboring
- Zealous laboring replacing pure consecration
- Having self-pity in the process of labor and growing

This book will explore these two groups and their resulting sideways paths and will explain them point by point. Dear brothers, I say again, on the path of following the Lord and serving Him, pay attention to "refusing to be common." We refuse the commonness in ourselves, and we refuse the things that are of Christ but replace Christ Himself. On the negative side, we refuse to be common; on the positive side, we press onward. May the Lord have mercy on us.

I

WORDS
OF A
WATCHMAN

Among the people on the earth, few believe in Jesus. Among those who believe in Jesus, few love the Lord. Among those who love the Lord Jesus, there are even fewer who can live well, live with value, and develop healthily. What is this valuable living? Just consider some of the admonishments in the Bible. The Lord commanded us to preach the gospel and to make disciples of all the nations. Through His servants, He encouraged us to stir up love, to labor diligently, and to serve single-mindedly. In the age of John's Revelation, the Lord still called out to the overcomers in the local churches, His testimonies. Who were the overcomers? They were those who refused to be common in their setting.

What a warning this is to us! It reminds us that not only must we believe in the Lord, but we also need to walk the narrow way in the reality of the cross. However, there are not many who walk this way. The Lord said, "Enter by the narrow gate; for wide is the gate and broad is the way that leads to destruction, and there are many who go in by it. Because narrow is the gate and difficult is the way which leads to life, and there are few who find it" (Matt. 7:13–14).

Terrible Loss among Christians

Just after Christians believe in the Lord, most have the desire to love Him and to live for Him. Yet it is hard to argue that many live up to the value they should have.

We have seen so many young ones love the Lord, but there are not many spiritual older brothers today. Why? What happened to all the young ones who loved the Lord and consecrated themselves to Him? Some eventually loved something other than the Lord Himself. Others were damaged by fleshly enjoyments or an unhealthy church life. As a result, they left the presence of the Lord, often unconsciously, and lost the supply of the heavenly life. They ceased enjoying the flow of life, and they became distant from the Lord whom they believed in.

Of course, they could perhaps be brought back to the Lord when they get older. Though such a return is wonderful, however, they have lost a valuable life, a life related to Christ. What a terrible waste this is! We must also say what a loss it is to the body of Christ. These ones could have become deacons who bless the church, strength to support the saints, or at least loving homes to care for the saints. They unknowingly lost it. This is indeed a warning for us!

Why do the Jesus lovers, especially the young ones, have this unfortunate experience? We may say that, in themselves, the following five principles are usually seen.

Lacking a Stern Face Toward Jerusalem

Concerning Jesus, the Bible says, "When the time had come for Him to be received up, that He steadfastly set His face to go to Jerusalem" (Luke 9:51, NKJV). The Lord Jesus had a stern face toward Jerusalem. He knew that humiliation, mockery, whipping, and even the cross were waiting for Him. However, He fixed His eyes on God alone and lived purely for God's desire. This was the source and strength for Him to live one with God.

We may love the Lord and faithfully consecrate to Him. However, for some reason, we are short of this kind of "stern" face. We are short of determination, of persistence, and of resolve. Besides God and Christ, we have too many other choices, plans, programs, and hopes for life. These are reasons why we become common.

Lacking the Being and Constitution of Acacia Wood

God desires to gain the valuable material of acacia wood. Growing in the midst of a desert, acacia wood is solid and doesn't rot. It also has thorns, signifying its ability to resist unhealthy things. Those who follow the Lord, lay hold of the Lord, and consecrate completely to the Lord must have this kind of being and constitution.

They won't be beaten by one incident.
They won't be pressed by some pain.
They won't be frustrated by difficulties.

When they say they are joined to the Lord, indeed they are joined to the Lord. They grow and become sturdy in Christ. At the same time, they can resist the things that damage them, and they fight against the temptations and attacks from Satan. They are serious and abide in their commitment. To them, the value of their existence is in God's desire. Their character insists on the good things, the things of the Lord, and their commitment from God. Without this kind of being and constitution of acacia wood, we will become common.

Being Self-centered

Another reason we become common and don't grow well is our self-centeredness. It is easy for us to get used to a particular life-style, environment, or way of living. We don't acknowledge that all of these things should be open to change.

A self-centered common man cannot accept changes. For example, when something changes in the church life, in the leading of the brothers, in spiritual companions, in working environments, or many other areas, the self-centered ones are filled with self-pity and self-love. They don't know how to obey God's hand, how to submit to the Lord's arrangement, and how to walk according to God's authority. Even if their self-centeredness is exposed, it is hard for them not to be common.

Not Respecting Marriage

Marriage is the most important thing for those who love the Lord. A common brother will quarrel with his wife because she doesn't meet his expectations, and he may even complain to the Lord. A common brother will compromise his stand if his spouse is dominating, and in turn he will lose the wisdom that comes from laying hold of the Lord. Or, a common man may love his wife "too much," worrying about things to the point that he loses his absoluteness unto the Lord.

A good marriage perfects a saint who loves the Lord.
A well-managed marriage helps a saint to grow.

A marriage with "one heart" produces restfulness. A marriage with "one spirit" blesses the church. A marriage with "one soul" becomes the support of the church. However, many brothers and sisters, even gifted and able ones, lose their value before God and become common simply because of how they lack respect for their marriage.

Overly Focusing on Personal Development

As we live our lives, we all want to have attainments. Christians, especially Jesus-lovers who hold a worldly job, should also have attainments and develop themselves. However, if they are not careful, their attainments and developments can become snares to make them not absolute to the Lord.

No one likes to live in poverty. Everyone would like to have a higher quality of living. However, having a "higher quality of living" has no limit. There is always a push to be richer, to have a higher position, and to become more respected. These may all seem meaningful, but all of these can rob away a gifted brother who loves the Lord and could be useful to the Lord.

If a brother is robbed away, a useful servant of the Lord will become a common brother, no different than any other person in the world. Although he may still love the Lord and serve according to his capacity, he is a "common" serving brother, speaker, or elder. He may consider himself to have the blessings of both heaven and earth, but actually, he has become common and has missed out on the hope God has for him.

PART 1

ONE WHO IS
NOT COMMON

01 / HAVING THE SPIRIT OF PIONEERING

An uncommon man manifests having the spirit of pioneering. In other words, he is a man of action. A passive man will do nothing even when the best chances come. But a man of action will take action at every opportunity. He will know how to utilize resources:

When he coordinates with a couple of saints, a gospel field can be cultivated.

When he serves in a church, many other churches can be affected.

The revelations and visions which he receives in Christ can bring in richer revelations and higher visions.

He is not a common man.

Looking at Earth from the Heavenlies

Today, we look at the heavenlies from our earthly perspective, but the Lord wants the opposite! He wants us to look at the earth from the heavenlies. This requires a broad soul. Brothers, to have such a view, you cannot have a small soul. You need to understand God's work over the whole earth so that you can cooperate with the Holy Spirit. For example, currently, one can see the financial investments in Africa are booming. If people can go to Africa for money, why can't you go for the testimony of the Lord?

Brothers need to receive the Lord's commitment to labor. For example, your place may have a few brothers and sisters together with two other families. If you know how to labor, the place will be blessed. Those who know how to labor bear fruit. But whether you know how to labor or not will depend on whether or not you are a man of action. **A common man simply maintains what is there, but a man of action will do pioneering work.**

Go, Pioneer!

This "pioneering spirit" is one of the best tests to see if we have become common, or ordinary. How do you know if you have become common? It is if you always feel, "This is good enough." An ordinary man is easily satisfied with the present situation. He will say, "Praise the Lord, we have enough people coming to the meeting." An ordinary man says this kind of word. But what kind of man is extraordinary? He who starts a new project and does pioneering work has an extraordinary mind.

Who is common? He who maintains.

Who has commitment? He who pioneers.

The Lord Jesus discipled the twelve apostles. They all were maintainers, including Peter. On the one hand, from the view of earth, the Lord's work needed to be maintained. The apostles preached the gospel, three thousand were saved (Acts 2:41) and then five thousand were saved (4:4). There were probably over ten thousand believers in Jerusalem at this time. How could the apostles leave? But on the other hand, from the heavenly perspective, the Lord had commanded them: "Go therefore and make disciples of all the nations" (Matt. 28:19a), even saying: "But you shall receive power when the Holy Spirit has come upon you; and you shall be witnesses to Me in Jerusalem, and in all Judea and Samaria, and to the end of the earth" (Acts 1:8). Therefore, the Lord raised up a hard environment in the church to "chase" the twelve apostles away. They simply couldn't stay. Eventually, even Peter left. When they left Jerusalem, they became very promising.

Think about it: if they stayed in Jerusalem, what was the eventual value? Even if they got tens of thousands more saved, what was the use? The Lord had not commanded them, "Stay in one street of Jerusalem and overlook ten thousand people." No! The Lord wanted them to go and be witnesses to the Lord, not only in Jerusalem, but also in all Judea and Samaria, and to the end of the earth.

Having a Commitment

If a servant of the Lord doesn't have the attitude, the mission, the assurance, but especially the commitment before the Lord, his serving will definitely be common.

However, the Lord desires to gain the extraordinary!

In church history, Europeans brought the gospel to China and generated some spiritual reality. This commitment created a group of spiritual men in Europe who were extraordinary. For example, I have always been impressed by Hudson Taylor, who founded the China Inland Mission. He was an extraordinary spiritual man. Another example was Theodore Austin-Sparks. He was also an extraordinary spiritual man. His spirituality was extremely high. (To you brothers, I say that being spiritual is a good thing, but if your spirituality is floating in the air and others don't understand what you say, this will not do. **Spiritual things should be presented in simple ways in order to help the saints.**)

Yes, we praise the Lord for these spiritual men whom He raised in Europe! Their work and their riches produced an extraordinary impact. The Lord sent some of them, like Hudson Taylor and Margaret Barber, to China to preach the gospel. Others, like T. Austin-Sparks, remained in Europe. But they all had their commitment and mission. The Lord set them forth as extraordinary examples for us!

02 / HAVING THE VIEW OF A GREAT SETUP

"Refusing to be common" is an attitude we must cultivate of not accepting our commonness. Some people are naturally uncommon, but for some reason, they remain common all their life! At the same time, others may be quite common naturally, but they can cultivate the attitude of "refusing to be common." This is just like me. I am actually very common, but I refuse to be common. Throughout my life, God has always given me a heart that said: **"Always fight! Always run!"** No matter how unpromising I am naturally, I don't compromise on the way of following the Lord.

Yes, I praise the Lord because of this! In principle, the world would never want a common man like me. However, in God's mercy, He sought me and chose me. Not only did He choose me, He also worked on me. I was a man of little use, but God made me useful, and I became a man refusing to be common.

Pioneering for the Lord's Testimony

Brothers, I hope all of you are more useful than me. To

do this, you must develop a desire to pioneer for the Lord's testimony. If you serve in a local church and feel, "This field is my world," you will easily become useless to the Lord. On the one hand, you should have a field, and it is okay to highly value this field for the sake of your labor. However, if you indulge this feeling, you will miss the view of pioneering.

If all the brothers in your locality can tell the Lord, "I will go preach the gospel to a European country in five years," or "I will raise up the Lord's testimony in an African country in five years," this is having a view of a great "setup," that is, a view of the great way in which the Lord's work could be planned and arranged.

With such a view, wouldn't the next five years be different in your church? In these five years, everyone could pray in one accord for one country and keep up a high morale. This is not common. This shows action! Yes, if brothers have this view to preach the gospel around the world in five years, it will result in positive action!

Our Labor Depends on the Setup

Brothers, we need to take action. We cannot stay ordinary. In action, our labor for the Lord will depend on the setup, our attitude, and the environment. We must resist having a small soul, just counting how many were in the church meeting that week: "We have ten more this week...we have eight less this week." Of course, there is nothing wrong with taking attendance in your meetings. However, if we have a small soul, we will do a small work, and our labor will ultimately be in a small field. Eventually, your soul will be ruined without realizing it.

To combat this, cultivate an open mind! Allow me to say something here to the elders. Many elders are nervous when they have a brother with talent and action who loves the Lord. Why are they nervous? It is because that brother is like "David," who can make the elders look like the incapable "Saul." At this time, elders may do things to push down this "David." No! Elders should have a large capacity and a broad mind.

Creating a Flow by Cooperating with the Holy Spirit in a Setup

Brothers, if you want to serve the Lord, you should have a high view, a broad mind, and solid spiritual equipment. If you don't have the solid spiritual equipment, you can never go on that far. More than this, you should have a higher level you are aiming at, a higher field you are looking to. If your setup and your consideration is always, "Ten more, fifteen more," it shows:

You don't know what a "flow" is; you only know how to labor.

You don't know what "the work of the Holy Spirit" is; you only know how to give yourself to work.

A man who understands labor desires to create a "flow." He desires to create a special labor environment. If you don't understand labor, you will simply work hard to circle a few people together. In the end, you will find that you are very common. However, a man who understands labor knows:

If the Holy Spirit gains five who love the Lord very much, I must labor with these five brothers and sisters to produce something.

Let me give you an illustration. In one locality, there was a fellowship meeting on Saturday evenings. One evening, a brother who seemed to be mentally unstable and with poor clothing came. He stood up in the meeting. Immediately, another brother went to stand with him and explained to the congregation, "This brother is limited both physically and psychologically. Recently, he touched the Lord. He desires to give himself to the Lord." Then, the limited brother knelt down and an elder laid hands on him to pray for him.

In reality, this brother's consecration had great limitation, but his desire touched many people. After the prayer, many brothers and sisters came up to give themselves to the Lord. What was this? It was a flow, created by the wise brother standing with the limited brother. The wise brother knew that the consecration of the limited brother, even though the consecration itself was limited, could bring in such a flow among the saints. For a time after that, every Saturday night meeting exhibited the work of the Holy Spirit. One family after another stood up to give testimonies of how they loved the Lord and were gained by the Lord, and the elders would pray for them. All of this is an illustration of good labor. They were not just working hard to gain a few people at their meetings. Instead, they were working with the Holy Spirit in their setup to create a flow.

Brothers, don't be common. Have a grand heart, have a great setup, have a broad mind, and remember the Lord's commitment to us: "Go therefore and make disciples of all the nations" (Matt. 28:19a). Don't think that you are doing okay where you are. Don't merely remain in one place. You must cultivate and develop a pioneering spirit!

03 / ENTERING THE NARROW GATE & WALKING THE DIFFICULT WAY

The Lord charged us to preach the gospel and make disciples of all the nations. He also encouraged us through His servants to stir up love, to labor diligently, and to serve single-mindedly. In the age of the book of Revelation, the Lord was still calling out to the overcomers in His testimonies, which are the local churches (Rev. 2–3).

Paul worked for the Lord and raised up local churches until he was martyred. In the end, the Lord chose the seven churches from Asia as various patterns for us, and He walked in the midst of the lampstands, the churches (Rev. 1:11–13). Think about these churches, which were probably all raised up by Paul. How many overcomers do you think were in each local church? To be honest, I think that if there were eight or ten overcomers in a local church, it would be very good.

The definition of an "overcomer" is relative to their setting. Perhaps someone who joins all the meetings is an overcomer because others don't go to meetings. Perhaps someone who goes to meetings and prays is an overcomer because though others go to the meetings, no one prays. Or perhaps someone who brings one person to salvation is an overcomer because no one else preaches the gospel.

Why was the Lord calling out overcomers in the age of the Revelation? It was because the church would one day be even more degraded, even to a point that was shocking. The fact that the Lord was calling for overcomers in the churches is a serious warning! It reminds us that **not only must we believe in the Lord, but we also need to walk the narrow way in the reality of the cross.**

However, there are not many who walk this narrow way. The Lord said, "Enter by the narrow gate; for wide is the gate and broad is the way that leads to destruction, and there are many who go in by it. Because narrow is the gate and difficult is the way which leads to life, and there are few who find it" (Matt. 7:13–14).

On one side is the wide gate and the broad way, which are easy to enter and walk on. On the other side is the narrow gate and difficult way, which are hard to find and difficult to walk on. This means you must pay a price to find the gate, and you must pay a price to walk the way. We may feel, "Yes Lord, I will do it!" But the Lord Himself said, "There are few who find it." Indeed, the eyes of the Lord run to and fro throughout the whole earth, looking for those He can support (2 Chr. 16:9; Zec. 4:10). This means He cannot find many. Most people are not who the Lord is looking for. Why? It is because they are too common to match the Lord's being.

Who can find the narrow gate and the difficult way? Those who are not common!

Who can the Lord find when His eyes run to and fro throughout the whole earth?

Those who are not common!

WORDS FROM THE HEART, WORDS OF TEACHING (1)

Yes, there are experiences that can damage brothers in the church. But overall, in principle, if you are damaged, it is because there is something in you that allows you to be damaged. Food does not hurt you; how you take the food can hurt you. If you are healthy, you know how to control yourself. But if you are overweight from overeating, you bear responsibility for how you took the food. Spiritually, no one can hurt you. If you are hurt, it is because you allowed yourself to be hurt.

Saul was a head taller than any of the people. He was a very impressive person. God anointed him; but eventually, God abandoned him because he departed from the original consecration.

The secret to being a good Christian is always speaking sweet words to the Lord, whether they are true or not. Whether you really love Him or not, learn to speak sweetly to Him. When you finish, just tell the Lord, "Lord, aren't You powerful? Make it all true."

Respect Marriage

Marriage is the most important thing in your life. It will decide whether you can serve the Lord well or not. Yes, whether you can serve the Lord well or not is decided not only by the Lord but also by your marriage.

If you decide to get married, you must be very clear that your spouse is given to you by the Lord. Once you are married, you must remember that love comes from God, whether you eventually like your spouse or not. You have to try your best to manage your marriage well. Before you get married, pray more, asking God for a suitable companion. After you get married, remember that this is the one whom God has given to you. Treat your spouse well.

A word for husbands—wives are easily satisfied. Just love her more. Do not criticize her shortcomings. Praise her virtues often. Tell her why you like her. God gave her to you for being heirs together of the grace of life (1 Pet. 3:7).

Purity

If you have a little impurity in your serving, you won't develop a ministry.

You serve the Lord because you love the Lord.

You cannot serve the Lord for developing something you consider valuable.

Without the Lord, all men are wicked. If you have other intentions besides the Lord, even a religious purpose for the Lord, you will become wicked. A little impurity in this way will cause you to try to attain your end goal by whatever means possible. If you go down this way, however, other young believers will lose faith in the church.

Vision and Testimony

The Bible encourages us to walk according to the patterns we see in other believers. You must take care that who you follow in the Lord is not based on brothers treating you well or not. If you follow someone because he treats you well, will you follow someone else when he treats you even better? No, you must have a clear vision: "I walk this way, I follow these brothers, because of the revelation the Lord has shown me!"

Why does God ask us to bear His testimony in a locality? It is for gaining a vessel to contain His riches in that locality.

I worry about leading ones losing their vision. If their vision is lost, they will care about people's needs instead of God's needs.

What is the difference between us and denominations? Most denominations operate according to people's needs—giving the messages people like, using the musical instruments people like, providing a social sphere people like, etc. If our church life is like this, it will become a social life in which the saints will be very distant from God. We should minister, function, and operate according to God's need. I hope the saints in the church life can know the Lord and His desire and that they can fight for the Lord's interests. This fighting would not be a matter of what is the "ground" or what is the "testimony"; it would be for the high and spiritual substance of the testimony.

Have the Lord; Touch the Lord

Why are you frustrated? It is because you don't know how to touch the Lord during critical moments. There are important moments in your life. For example, dating is an important moment. Functioning in the church is an important moment. Ministering is an important moment. At these moments, if you don't know how to have the presence of the Lord, you will face the situation yourself and end up making decisions by yourself.

You may be zealous. You may serve the Lord. You may work for Christ. However, you may be short of the presence of the Lord. Because of that, you won't have the strength to face difficulties. When a particular situation arises, you will feel difficult and frustrated. You must therefore develop a skill of coming to the presence of the Lord.

You may endeavor to go to all the meetings, but do you have the Lord in all your activities? If you don't have much of the Lord, your inner life will be weak. Following the Lord is ultimately related to the inner life. You must be able to ask the Lord, "Why are you breaking me?" And you must be able to hear His answer: "It is for My will. This is the only way for you to be transformed and conformed to the image of Christ."

Treasure Hymns

You need to treasure hymns. Hymns are one of the best helps along the way of following the Lord.

Hymns with sensations but without depth will give you a good feeling. However, this kind of hymn cannot help you grow, cannot help you to be intimate with the Lord, and cannot help you go through difficulties.

Hymns are spiritual milk, the cream of spiritual people's experiences throughout the generations of Jesus lovers. You need hymns with depth and substance, for these hymns are like warm milk that brings the Lord's presence to you.

Music has no distinction between sacred and secular.

Music is just music. It is good as long as it brings you to the presence of the Lord.

If you have recently had a hymn in your heart, you should learn to sing and memorize a few lines to be your prayer. This exercise will help you develop your life relationship with the Lord.

Love God according to God

Try your best to understand when I say this: the Lord is "selfish." He knows that our only hope is that He would be selfish. If He is not selfish, we will have no way to go because we are too shallow. We are just common fallen men. No matter how much we desire the Lord, our life is so low. However, brothers and sisters, are you a Christian for yourself, or for God? We must be elevated, live a high-standard Christian life, and love God according to God.

The Bible doesn't say that God is selfish. It only says that He is jealous (Exo. 20:5; Deut. 4:24; 2 Cor. 11:1–4). If we want anything, gain anything, or go anywhere according to our own standards, He is not happy. He is jealous that we would want anything besides Himself. How does this apply to our lives? Take the examples of our children or our parents. We must love them. However, I would ask how we must love them. When we love our children and parents according to God, He is joyful. If we don't love them according to God, He will be jealous.

If we walk according to our own low standard, we will go nowhere. If we walk according to God, we will advance and be saturated in the divine realm. In this realm, God is everywhere. A hymn says, "And everywhere be Thee and God." It means that no matter where we go, God is there. He saturates our whole being and brings us to His satisfaction. We are able to forsake the world and only gain God Himself!

The Subjective Experience of Life

Whether or not we know it or care, it is a historical fact that Christ died on the cross. However, if we don't take the cross of Christ into our hearts, the effect will not apply to us.

Spiritual truth is special. You must enter into its reality so that the truth can be constituted in you and applied in you. This is true in the beginning of the Christian life. It is also true in our daily life from that day forward.

The cross of Christ shouldn't be a picture on your wall. You must take it into your heart. Without the subjective experience of the cross, the Bible won't affect you and the death and resurrection of Christ will mean nothing to you. Similarly, all the important things in the Christian life should be like this. They must become your subjective experience in life.

Love and Knowledge

There is a hymn that says, "To bring thee to thy God, love takes the shortest route; the way which knowledge leads, is but a roundabout."

If you are led by knowledge in your Christian life, you will be lost on a roundabout.

The shortest route to gain God is to love Him.

After you love the Lord, knowledge will help you appreciate the Lord more.

Love is the foundation of the relationship between you and the Lord.

Tell the Lord, "Lord, I love You. Because I love You, I would like to be more equipped in my knowledge of you. However, Lord, this equipping is only for me to love You more."

Seminaries teach mostly knowledge related to God, to Jesus, to salvation, and to serving. In the end, the life element may disappear. However, God is for us to love. The closer we are to God, the more we love Him. The more you love Him, the more you have Him. The more you love Him, the more you know Him. This love should increase and become richer, fuller, and deeper. If our knowledge surpasses our love, it loses its value.

When you go to a meeting and listen to a message, you should enjoy the anointing and the presence of the Lord. This is what helps you get closer to the Lord and love the Lord more, not the knowledge conveyed in the message. Guard yourself against being fascinated by new knowledge, since no matter how new it is, it will eventually become old and stale. However, love for God will turn all knowledge of Him into your reality.

Foundation

In your life, you will face situation after situation, problem after problem, difficulty after difficulty, and choice after choice. At those moments, you need Christ and the word of the Lord. Without the Lord Himself and the Bible as your foundation, it will be hard for you to make proper decisions.

The Lord would like to work on you, but you need a proper foundation for this work. In other words, you need a good foundation in order to answer His leading. Without such a foundation, you cannot follow His leading.

I always feel that we are like owners of a dollar store. Making small deals makes us happy. We don't want to be challenged. If you don't challenge yourself and challenge what you know or have heard, the things which you thought you had won't be yours. However, if you don't have a solid foundation and begin to challenge, this challenging will hurt you and prevent you from properly growing.

Do not challenge carelessly. You need to ask whether a challenge will bring you reality or not. For example, the Lord's Table is a good practice. You don't need to challenge it or deny it. Rather, you need to ask yourself, "Do I have the reality of the Lord's Table? Do I recognize this meeting as the element of the church, for we have one Lord, one body, one cup, and one bread?"

Eventually, your development depends on what you have. How much you produce will be based on how solid your foundation is. If you are familiar with the Bible, the Bible can speak to you, and when some brothers help you to see points from the Bible, you will be able to apply these points. One day, the truth you received will match the word from brothers and begin to blossom.

If you don't build a solid foundation for your Christian life, God cannot work on you and you will not develop. Basic truths should be solid in you. When you try to develop without such a foundation, it is actually very dangerous.

You must also have a good foundation to develop new things. If you don't care about your foundation and just want to go forward, you won't have much real hope or a way to go on.

PART 2

TURNING TO A SIDEWAY BECAUSE OF OURSELVES

GETTING LOST BY
DRIFTING "GRADUALLY"

Just after Christians believe in the Lord, most have the desire to love Him and to live for Him. However, not many live their Christian life well and develop the value which they should have before the Lord.

Time is the Best Servant of the Lord

We have seen so many young ones love the Lord, but there are not many spiritual older brothers today. Why? What happened to all the young ones who loved the Lord and consecrated themselves to Him? Some eventually loved something other than the Lord Himself. Others were damaged by fleshly enjoyments or an unhealthy church life. As a result, they left the presence of the Lord, often unconsciously, and lost the supply of the heavenly life. They ceased enjoying the flow of life, and they became far away from the Lord whom they believed in.

Brothers, worldly enjoyment can damage you, but even the church life can damage you if you are not careful. At a certain point, you may ask yourself, "Is this worthwhile? Is it worthwhile for me to give my all to this?" Many young ones were vital and loved the Lord in the beginning. In the end, they disappeared. Some loved the world. Some pursued worldly enjoyments. Some were disappointed by the quarrels in the church life. I remember when I had just began to love the Lord, the Holy Spirit worked strongly in the church. Many brothers and sisters loved the Lord at that time. Now, these ones have left one after another, and not many are still in the church life.

This is why I say time is the best servant of the Lord.

The real situations of many brothers and sisters are manifested through time.

Perhaps these ones will be brought back when they get older. However, they have lost a valuable life, a life related to Christ. What a terrible waste it is! They could have become a deacon who blesses the church, a strength to support the saints, or a loving home to care for the saints. They lost this value unknowingly. This is indeed a warning for us!

Becoming Lost without Realizing It

Brothers, people get lost without realizing it. Don't think, "Hey, what's wrong with getting a job?" For some brothers, it is okay to have a job. However, for some brothers, it may not be okay. One brother testified, "I tried my best to get my company listed on the stock exchange. I thought I would have more time after it was listed. However, I am much busier than before. I thought I would be freer when I had more money, but I am actually much busier after that."

It is not scary that a man has weaknesses and limitations. What is scary is when he starts to drift away a little today, a little farther one month later, and even farther one year later. After three years, his Lord will seemingly "disappear." Brothers, if you are this one, **you don't even know that your Lord has disappeared, and you are lost.** Oh, we need to be watchful. Anything that causes us to drift in such a way is damaging to our relationship with the Lord. We have to refuse it when "damage" comes. We need to say, "No, I don't want it."

Genesis tells us that Lot, Abraham's nephew, dwelt in the cities of the plain after leaving Abraham, and that he eventually pitched his tent even as far as Sodom (Gen. 13:12b). Sodom represented the lowest place on earth at that time. How did Lot get there? He **"gradually"** moved his tent and eventually reached Sodom. I believe Lot did this without even realizing it. Many Christians who love Jesus also become lost gradually without realizing it.

Not Knowing Why We are Unable to Face the Lord

There was a brother who invited another brother to do business with him. He said, "You only need to spend two hours a week, and we will offer ten percent of the profit to the church." This sounded so good to the second brother that it was hard to turn it down. However, eventually he had to spend forty and even sixty hours a week instead of the original promise of two. This brother promised to finish his part in two months, but in fact it went on and on. I have heard so many people say, "This will only take one year," or, "I will be busy for only half of the year." Actually, brothers, this is never true!

If we cannot face the Lord, it will not be because one day we were determined to love the world or to commit a sin. No! If we love the world or commit a sin, the Lord will surely immediately tell us, "No! Repent!" and we can come back to Him. If we can't face the Lord when in His presence, it will be without us even knowing why. Maybe after two years, we will feel, "What am I doing?" Maybe after we retire, we finally come back to the Lord and love Him. However, we will have lost our function and our lifetime value.

A servant of the Lord needs to be careful from the very beginning. Do not get lost "without knowing why." Don't think, "I will just try this once and it will be okay." No, you will be away from the Lord and eventually get lost.

05 LACKING A STERN FACE FACING JERUSALEM

Lacking a Stern Face Facing Jerusalem

Why do so many Jesus lovers, especially the younger ones, experience drifting away? We may say that they lack a stern face facing Jerusalem.

For most people, it is hard to have a stern face. Most of us hope for a pleasant face. However, our Lord had a stern face as He faced Jerusalem, which indicated, "I will be martyred. This is My life. I refuse any opposition!" He knew that humiliation, mockery, whipping, and even the cross were waiting for Him. However, He "faced Jerusalem," which means He set Himself toward God's interests. He fixed His eyes on God alone and lived purely for God's desire. This was the source and strength for Him to live one with God.

Watchman Nee gave a message called "The Path Leading to Glory" talking about the Lord going all the way to Jerusalem. Brother Nee knew the meaning of "facing Jerusalem," which is, "Lord, I lay hold of You, I cling only to You, and I am absolutely for You." He said in his message, "We lay hold of the Lord and behold Him. We don't want anything else. We don't desire anything else. We refuse everything else. We know that mockery and humiliation are waiting ahead. But our future is glory!" He also wrote a hymn saying:

My glory's in the coming age,
Today I'll patient be.
I'd ne'er enjoy ahead of Him
This world's prosperity.

This absoluteness for the Lord and His desire is the "stern face facing Jerusalem" so many lack.

Clinging to the Lord versus Being Moved by Others

We may love the Lord and faithfully consecrate to Him. However, we do not cling to the Lord enough. Besides God and Christ, we have too many other choices, plans, programs, and hopes for life. These are reasons why we become common.

Once, a brother who loved the Lord very much told his parents and teachers he wanted to serve the Lord. He testified with tears, "My family asked me, is this what your life is going to be?" His teachers also asked him, "You believe in Jesus. What will you do with your life? Is your life going to be like this?" His testimony was very touching, even I cannot forget it. However, although he had paid a big price to follow the Lord, he couldn't continue. He left the Lord because his parents, friends, teachers, and classmates were against him.

You ask, "Did he sin?" No. "Did he love the world?" No. However, I believe he is "lost." Gradually, he drifted away from the Lord and became far from Him. At the time of his testimony, he wanted to serve the Lord. But without laying hold of and clinging to the Lord enough, he was lost.

Brothers, we will become common, taking a side way, when we follow the Lord based on our human relations. For example, what do you do if your father is against you loving the Lord? Your teachers want you to progress and get a PhD, but when you have such a degree and a good future, can you serve the Lord full-time? It is not easy. Human relations have come in. People give you their own advice and affect your decision for the Lord.

Let me give another illustration (one that will feel more relevant to United States immigrants). Suppose you have made the decision to serve full-time when, suddenly, someone tells you that there is a good job opportunity in New York City. They can help you get a green card and stay in the U.S. Your heart may be stirred, and you may think the Lord has opened a way for you. Brothers, we are easily persuaded by others and end up walking sideways.

Focusing on the Lord in Making Decisions

Lacking a stern face facing Jerusalem shows that we are not firm. Not focusing on Christ in making decisions shows that we only consider ourselves. However, a servant of the Lord must face Jerusalem. His face must be stern: "I am for Christ and for the church absolutely all my life!" He must follow the Lord firmly, recognizing this is the best and the most valuable way. He only focuses on the Lord, even neglecting other voices and opinions to just follow the Lord. He says:

> "I have no future. I have no career. I have no hope.
> I only recognize Jesus, who is Christ.
> **The one I follow is Jesus Christ.**
> I am His servant. I am His maidservant. **I must lay hold of Him all my life!**
>
> I don't have my own choices, my own plans, my own program, or my own hope for life."

Some may sit at the end of their lives atop piles of money and sigh, "This is it. I can leave now." However, we are different. We sit in the presence of the Lord and proclaim with the breath of life, "I have fought the good fight, I have finished the race, I have kept the faith" (see 2 Tim. 4:7). This process requires steadfastness.

Drifting to Vanity

Brothers, you possibly don't realize how hard it is to "face Jerusalem"! On the way of following the Lord, sin is waiting for every one of us. Every sin has a sign above it, reading: "A Golden Chance from Heaven," and moves your heart. You may have originally faced Jerusalem: you only desired God, you were for only God, and you only followed God. Then, for some reason, you see such a sign and drift down a side path to vanity and to curse. You can lose your sternness toward the Lord without realizing it. You will still say, "Lord, I am

Yours," but at the same time, you will begin to plan how to do business and develop your career.

Brothers, what does it take to sternly face Jerusalem? It means you won't follow people when they talk about money or the things of the world. It means you take care of the consecration in your heart to only lay hold of the Lord and to walk to the end of the Lord's way. You must be firm: "I only desire the Lord. I am only to satisfy the Lord. I just want to follow the Lord. I will walk facing Jerusalem all my life!" At the times you can declare this, you have a stern face in the Lord's mercy. I hope we all can tell this to the Lord, with a feeling of, "Lord, I want to be Your match. I want to serve You faithfully."

A WORD FROM THE HEART, ABOUT CHARACTER

Our life is ultimately determined by one thing—not our talent or our intelligence, but our character. To illustrate, I know an old brother who is very disciplined. In fact, I have never seen anyone who is more disciplined than him. He is very strict on himself. His desk, his clothes, everything is neat one hundred percent. When he heard the gospel and was saved, he gave himself absolutely to the Lord right away. We are different. We heard the Lord's calling to consecrate ourselves when we got saved. We said "Amen!" easily, and then we disappeared. The Lord had to call us again. This is related to character. Some people are loose, while others, like the old brother, are disciplined. Some people are sober. When they want to read the Bible, they read the Bible seriously. Some are diligent. When they want to preach the gospel, they preach faithfully.

Brothers, your character will eventually decide your life. Good character generates stability. Good character generates strength. Good character allows you to pursue desperately to reach the goal. Good character is something beyond success or failure. Whether a man is a good Christian or not, if he has good character, he is ready to accept the Lord's challenge and will insist on finishing it.

On the difficult pathway of following the Lord, you will face many changes, limitations, and frustrations. Good character will help you go through all these experiences, because your character allows you to be firm for the Lord's commitment. You won't leave for just any reason. I will say this again and again: The question of whether someone can be used by the Lord is very much answered by what kind of character he or she possesses.

Training your character means to train yourself to be "genuine, exact, strict, diligent, broad, fine, stable, patient, deep," and so on. Yet in principle, character is very hard to train, because it is related to your being. Your being is who you are. No one can change their being, and it is their being that will mold or restrict their character. Some people are "small," and everything bothers them. Some people are "broad," and nothing bothers them. This should be our learning.

However, though it is very hard to train your character, you still need to try. If you don't try to train yourself, you won't know how hard such training is. Once you realize this, you will appreciate it whenever you encounter good character. Eventually, when you develop your ministry, good character will be a great help to this development. Whether or not you can be a servant of the Lord depends on your character.

06 / LACKING ADVANCEMENT

The most fearful thing for a serving one is to become common, having no advancement. For example, a brother may be good at writing hymns but he becomes common. Why? He only acknowledges his own hymns and promotes his own hymns no matter where he goes. He only stays in his hymns. He never tells the Lord, "I want to advance." Therefore, he becomes common.

There were two young coworkers. They learned the way I preached, including my tone and the gestures I used when ministering. It was good, but they didn't realize that it is easy to learn a skill but hard to learn "the person." They didn't realize that someone fighting for the Lord will insist on advancing, no matter how tired he is. If we are uncommon and advance and develop, there will be a great land for us to pioneer.

Some brothers have repeatedly told me, "Peace and restfulness is to be valued most." I tell them, "Peace shouldn't be valued most. Christ is to be valued most." To serve the Lord, we shouldn't value peace most, we should value Christ and gaining Him. To walk in the pathway of the Lord, we must advance. We can never compromise. We can never find an "easy way" to survive! No! This is not the way to serve the Lord. If you have this kind of attitude, it reveals that you are common. A common man just wants to survive; an uncommon man looks to advance.

Staying In One Place, Marching In Place

What I worry most for you brothers is becoming common. A man of action will speak to a mountain blocking him, "I will drill a tunnel through you!" Yes, if the Lord commands you, you must be able to say, "Even being against thousands, I shall go forward anyway." This is the mindset of advancing.

An advancing man always has a higher plan. **He doesn't stay in one place or march in place.** He seeks to uplift himself and to lead the church to be uplifted. Brothers, especially the young ones, on the one hand, you must be stable. If you are not stable, who dares to have hope in you or trust you? On the other hand, if others can have hope in you and trust you, you must also become an advancing man.

Those who are not advancing will focus on "our congregation has increased from fifteen to twenty" in one place. Is this good? Of course it is good. To preach the gospel and get people saved is good. However, if you have twenty people this year, thirty people next year, and forty the year after, what can you do when you are forty years old? One elder said, "Even at my age, I still have a congregation to shepherd. Praise the Lord." He doesn't realize that his mindset is common and that he is not advancing!

Not Producing, Not Developing

Those who are advancing will be able to produce something. A Chinese general once said, "Most people are common. They look for one or two leaders, and then love to follow them." A lot then depends on those leaders. If a serving one or a leading one is fighting to advance, the saints they are with will gain more.

Some brothers are too smart and calculate the loss and gain in everything. Some brothers seem foolish, but they are pioneering. One brother drove six hours to visit some brothers, but he didn't find anyone. Praise the Lord for his trying. The principle of his work is refusing to be common.

Just because you are refusing to be common doesn't mean that you will produce someone uncommon. Even an uncommon man can produce something quite common. We should strive that what we produce also bears the marks of fighting commonness.

"Not being common" is to develop more testimonies of the Lord with the capital that the Lord has given you. Very few fight for this kind of thing.

Brothers, I urge you to look at the world map. Pray for one city, one region, or even one country. Perhaps the goal is too big to achieve, but I believe the Lord can have His pioneering work in any place. It just depends on how we do it.

Having a Narrow View
or a Limited Plan

Brothers, be advancing, otherwise we are too common. Bringing five people to salvation in five years is very good, but even this goal is too small. We who are serving the Lord cannot waste our time. We cannot become good for nothing.

I hope you brothers can be advancing and promising with a heart of pioneering the globe. I hope you cultivate yourselves for this goal. If you don't know how to cultivate yourself, tell the Lord, "Cultivate me, Lord." And then pick up a burden to pioneer. As a result, your capacity will be broadened. You will have a grander view and dream. However, take care not to be flashy without substance. Do not reach for what is beyond your grasp. Learn the local language, learn to preach the gospel, and learn to minister for the Lord. Yet without a bigger plan, we will be common. May the Lord have mercy on us.

A WORD FROM THE HEART, ABOUT FIELDS (1)

One of the reasons young men cannot develop is older ones don't let go. **It is important for the older ones to know both how to let go and how to protect the young ones from going astray at the same time.** After brothers have pursued the Lord for one year, only a few will serve the Lord full-time; most will go back to their locality. These brothers will face a problem: the leading ones will not give them a field of labor for them to develop.

After trainings like this, many brothers quiet down when they go back to their locality. Some even stop going to meetings. It is because they don't have a field. The church doesn't know how to bless them. The leading ones only want these brothers to bless the church and cooperate with the structure of the church. It doesn't work. We shouldn't ask people to cooperate with the structure of the church. We shouldn't control people in this way. We should desire brothers to serve the Lord freely.

"I Have a Field"

I am very blessed. I began to love the Lord when I was in high school. I joined the church's high school meeting and served the children. Every Lord's Day, I went to the meeting hall early in the morning. Some brothers read the Bible with me and taught me how to share. Then I went to teach the children. I learned a lot through this experience. I learned how to be with brothers, how to follow the brothers' leading, and how to tell Bible stories to children. All this learning was because I had a field—the children's meetings.

Later, I went to Hall 27 of the church in Taipei. This is called "a field." There were mostly older saints there, so I was asked to speak at the meetings. I didn't know what to do, so I gave the messages of "Twelve Baskets Full" by Brother Nee at the Lord's Day meetings. During the week, I preached the gospel to such an extent that the little kids would call out, "Jesus is coming!" when they saw me walking. One time, I visited an older brother who was a battalion commander. He said, "Brother Chu, you are my father." I was shocked and didn't know what to say. He showed me the verse, "for in Christ Jesus I have begotten you through the gospel" (1 Cor. 4:15). Since my gospel preaching had saved him, he said, I was his father. I wept when I heard this and felt I was unworthy. I was only a twenty-two-year-old young man. It was because of the Lord's mercy that I could speak for Him, fight for Him, and visit the saints, and that the hall could be a field for me to develop. At that time, I had a feeling that this was my life: by honor and dishonor, by evil report and good report; as deceivers, and yet true; as unknown, and yet well known (2 Cor. 6:8–9a).

Then, I went to my first university in a small town. There was only a small meeting hall. I preached the gospel and had a meeting. The church had about twenty-five or thirty people, but through gospel preaching, we brought in fifteen more. With more people coming in, I had a field.

Brothers, I share my story to illustrate to you: **you will grow when you have a field.**

If you don't want to be common, you need to have a field. Without a field, no one can develop.

Learn to develop yourself in everything. Learn how to pray, how to lead, how to fellowship, how to preach the gospel, how to arrange hospitality, and so on. Cultivate yourself through your field.

Develop Basic Skills for Surviving

Brothers, if you have a burden to pioneer a new city, a new state, or a new country for the Lord, you need to first develop some basic "survival skills."

Boy Scouts are trained in some basic ways to survive in difficult environments. We need the same thing for our spiritual life. Spiritual survival skills are what allowed me to survive spiritually when I had just arrived in the U.S. decades ago. What are these skills? You must learn to bring people to salvation, to lead a Bible study, and to have spiritual companions. These are some basic survival skills.

Brothers, do not waste your life. You need to have a field and operate in it. Help people get saved and love the Lord. Become a spiritual parent for the weaker and younger saints. Take care of them, help them, and encourage them so that they become a strength to bless the church. Learn to help brothers love one another and to come together in a sweet way. When people see you together, they can see your joy and your smile.

More than this, learn to work things out. Don't wait for others to tell you what to do. In this way, you will learn more. Don't be bound. You should be free in your planning, even though it may not make any sense. If people laugh at you when you talk about things, you should tell them, "Brothers, do not laugh at me. Although I can't speak it out very well, it is from the Lord. It is not for you to laugh at."

Create Your Own Field

Brothers, remember: have a field, no matter what. Leading hymns can be a field. Preaching the gospel can be a field. The church life can be a field. Church meetings can be a field. Everyone deserves a field, and almost anything can be a field. It all depends how you treat it. For this reason, we need to have a spirit to fight for every single saint. Do not be too smart. We may think someone is not qualified, another is not good enough, this one cannot develop, or that one is not hopeful. No. No one knows their future.

Learn to create a field and develop. For example, how do you develop a meeting? Do not just rely on an old way: Sing a few hymns and then a brother gives a message. You should find a way to let every brother function. Help two or three brothers. Then, you four brothers can help twelve people. Everyone can be ready to speak in the meeting.

The Lord told us, "And whoever compels you to go one mile, go with him two" (Matt. 5:41). In fact, it is the Lord who asks you to go one mile with Him; are you willing to go two miles? For example, the Lord could ask you to "preach the gospel." You could do the activity, or you could do extra and equip yourself, becoming "a man who is good at preaching the gospel." How? You pray more. You memorize at least twenty verses in order to preach the gospel, like "For there is one God" (1 Tim. 2:5), "For with the heart one believes unto righteousness, and with the mouth confession is made unto salvation" (Rom. 10:10), "Jesus said to her, 'I am the resurrection and the life. He who believes in Me, though he may die, he shall live'" (John 11:25), and so on. This is far more than simply carrying a task or activity. This is to "walk two miles," and in doing so, you have created a field.

Let me illustrate with another example. A brother could work in one city but also have a burden to preach the gospel in a new city. This is walking with the Lord an extra mile. If you live before the Lord like this, your potential fields will be endless.

Do not become a pastor in one place. Do not be just for one city. If you are like this, your field will be gone. However, if you are for people, the field will be wide open. If you say, "I want to memorize Galatians this year," the field will be gone. If you say, "I want to know the Bible more this year," the field opens up. Fields come not by our carrying out a task, but by how we consider ourselves and what we have.

Brothers and sisters, we should pray, "Lord, I appreciate this kind of freedom. I appreciate the opportunities You give. I want to be faithful. I want You to have Your way on the earth. Oh, cultivate me, work on me, and develop me!"

A WORD FROM THE HEART, ABOUT FIELDS (2)

Brothers, you must have a field, you must labor in your field, and you must make it productive. If you don't want to be common, you need such a field. However, let me say this:

Do you need to have a field? Yes.
Do you need to avoid remaining in a field? Yes.
That is correct. Both answers are "yes."

A field allows us to grow, develop, and develop even more. However, **we cannot remain in that field.** Let me give my own example. I learned a lot in Taiwan. When I came to the U.S., I was quite experienced. I knew how to preach the gospel, how to give a message, how to visit saints, how to care for patients at the hospital, and I even had the gift of healing. Praise the Lord, I didn't become addicted to it. I wasn't occupied by my field. If I was occupied, I would have become zealous in my work for the Lord but forget the Lord Himself. I would have focused on how many were in the meeting and how many got saved. This would eventually have harmed me and made me common.

Brothers, if you are occupied by your field, you will eventually become very common. You will say, "I have my church. I have my ministry. I have a commitment from the Lord. I have my serving in the church. I have my assignment from the elders." These are all fields. However, when we have a field, we easily replace Christ with that field. For some reason, the Lord becomes far from us and the field becomes so important. We begin to have our "territory." Yes, we should protect those whom we brought to salvation, just like parents protect their children. However, you shouldn't be faithful to the field without Christ. **You must not be occupied by a field.**

Bearing Fruit, Raising Up Pillars

If you are occupied by a field and it becomes your "territory," others will become frustrated. We must understand that the value of our serving depends on two things, and the others are not important.

First, are you fruitful? In other words, are people saved through you?

Second, can you raise up pillars?

Don't talk so much about how to have good administration, good meetings, a good Lord's Table, or how the saints love one another. I will just ask you two things: first, do you have fruit when you preach the gospel? Second, are you able to raise up some of your fruit to be pillars, upholding the church life? Fruitfulness is important to pay attention to, because it reveals that someone is burdened. We all have relatives and friends. If the Lord touches you, they will be in your heart and you will have a burden for their salvation and to help them get saved. Then, you can develop more.

Yet only bearing fruit is not enough. There is still the

second question: are you able to raise up pillars? One day, if something happens to you or to the church, the going on of the church will very much be related to pillars, not to your fruitfulness. With pillars, the church can go on no matter what happens. At the same time, any brother who is a pillar or who has some "pillar element" can move anywhere and begin to care for some new ones. The testimonies of the Lord can still be raised up in different localities through the movement of pillars.

Pillars: Those with Stature and Riches

Who are pillars?
Those who have spiritual stature and spiritual riches are the pillars. Many Jesus-lovers have riches, but without stature.

How are pillars raised up?
The stature of pillars is grown through good perfecters (the gifts in the church), good soil (a proper setting), and a solid foundation (the right learning).

The Bible tells us both to be rooted and to grow unto the measure of the stature of the fullness of Christ (see Col. 2:6–7; Eph. 4:13–14). We cannot just "grow tall." We need to have the right stature. This growth requires good soil, which is based on our environment. When we grow in good soil, we need to develop a good stature. Do not just fulfill religious duty. Try your best to grow, to sprout in rich soil, and to produce riches. Pursue, labor, and receive the help of the brothers' riches so that you may become rich.

Because of the help of the apostles, prophets, evangelists, and the gifts whom God has given to the church (Eph. 4:11–12), you can grow tall unto the measure of the stature of the fullness of Christ. These are the proper pillars, those who have both stature and riches. For these ones, the taller they get, the richer they are.

One of the biggest dangers to raising up pillars is the "mixed multitude." Actually, they are the most troublesome group of people in the church life. When Moses led the Israelites out of Egypt, there was "a mixed multitude" among them (Exo. 12:38; Num. 11:4). This group is opinionated and cannot develop. If the "mixed multitude" in the church life becomes too large or too strong, the church life will become chaotic or even collapse (see Matt.13:33; 1 Cor. 5:6). Then, there is no chance for the church to develop pillars with stature and riches.

Fruit is Strengthened by Pillars

You can go out to preach the gospel and bear fruit. Everyone needs to have fruit. After people are saved, however, how do they depart from their old lifestyle and how can they pass through difficulties? It very much depends on the presence of pillars who have the strength to support.

You may say a brother is problematic. Let me ask you: are there any brothers who are advancing but not problematic? You may say a brother gives you a headache. Let me ask you: are there any brothers who have a burden but don't give you a headache? Many saints come to the meetings. They just sit there and greet you nicely. They bring food for the love feast and offer money. They don't give you any headaches. However, except for growing some gray hair and wrinkles, after thirty years they remain the same!

Only those who are advancing with a burden can become pillars. Not all can go this way. For example, say one hundred people are saved through us. It is impossible for these one hundred people to all become pillars. We hope that ten percent, five percent, or even three percent can become pillars. The outcome of fruit overall and the future of the church depends on such pillars.

The Secret of Being a Pillar: Ignore the Imperfections

Brothers, I have loved the Lord for sixty years. By the Lord's mercy, I have grown and have a certain stature with riches even though I also have my limitations. No one is without limitation. If you say you have no limitation, it is because you are too young and the Lord has dared not expose you yet. If you really follow the Lord, you will be like a tree with knots (these knots are your limitations). If you don't grow, there will be no knots, but you also will not be a blessing to the church. I can assure you: when you grow and become a blessing to the church, you will have knots. Little trees don't have knots. Only big old trees have knots. Therefore, do not long to be "perfect."

If the Lord wants to use you, He must show that you are not perfect. If the more we grow, the more we see how imperfect we are, then how can we stand before the Lord for His desire? **The secret to being a pillar in the presence of the Lord is to ignore our imperfections.** When you read the biographies of spiritual men, you will find out that all of them had problems, both big and small. However, God is so grand that He allows such problems to exist. God seems to be jealous. He doesn't want you to be perfect. He only desires to show Himself to be the Savior. If you are perfect while you are living, people will treat you like a savior. No. We only have one Savior—Jesus. Only He is flawless and perfect.

Brothers, we need to have a strong desire: "I want to bear fruit. I will talk to people on the street about Jesus. I will go to the food court on campus to preach the gospel. I want to have fruit!" After you bear fruit, the most important thing then is to raise up pillars. To raise up pillars is more hidden than fruit bearing, but more crucial. The churches desperately need pillars that can support the testimony of the Lord. We need brothers who are perfected to be pillars. All who serve the Lord must try their best to help the brothers who are with them to be pillars to support God's testimony instead of simply being good brothers.

07

LACKING THE BEING & CONSTITUTION OF ACACIA WOOD

As we talk about not being common, we need to mention our being and constitution. Our being is related to our personality. Some people are too emotional and some are too smart. These are personalities. Let me share my own example. I am an emotional person, but the Lord worked on me, and I gradually developed my will. Now, I have the personality of "absoluteness." I am absolute unto the Lord. I can endure many situations and I don't pity myself. This is my personality, which is my being.

Allowing God to Work and Produce a Useful Being

He who is useful in God's hand has allowed God to hammer him. God's hammering work is for you to become a useful vessel. However, in the process, we often run from or refuse the hammered work and thus lose our proper function.

He who can be used by the Lord must be able to stand for the Lord. This standing is not easy. It requires a price. If God wants to gain a person, He will say, **"There is no easy way!"** The Lord cannot use those who have too much occupying their mind, who are too fussy, who are too smart, or who are too shrewd. The Lord doesn't use those who are naturally honest and solid either. He says, **"I only use those I have worked on."** Yes, the Lord can only use those who give themselves completely to the Lord, allowing God not only to bear their responsibilities but also to work on them.

It is not an easy matter for a man to be worked upon by God. Watchman Nee wrote a hymn about God's working:

How harshly, mightily must Thy rod strike,
*   to drink obtain?*
To what hot blaze must Thy fire be raised
*   till trials are complete?*
How deep, how painfully must Thy thorn pierce,
*   till there's an outflow sweet?*

*   — "Sometimes Even a Blue Sky"*

Brothers, God wants to use us. He is willing to use us; but we have our limitations. There are many Jesus lovers, but not everyone can be useful. We must go through the work of God's hands. Some brothers are talented and able. Their talent and ability need God's work so that they can become a precious vessel to be used by God.

As you labor, your deductions will be based on your capacity. The deeper your being is, the better your deduction will be. If you are shallow, your deduction will also be shallow. **The most difficult thing is to face a significant situation.** Just coping with a situation "for the time being" is a worse way, because it is a way without any hope in the future.

Acacia Wood is Strong and Resistant

Those who have the Lord must allow Him to work with their constitution. The Lord would like to constitute each one of us with the constitution of acacia wood. Many times, our commonality comes because we don't have both the being and constitution of acacia wood. God desires valuable material, and this material is acacia wood.

In the building of the tabernacle, acacia wood was used greatly. God told Moses, "And they shall make an ark of acacia wood; two and a half cubits shall be its length, a cubit and a half its width, and a cubit and a half its height... And you shall make poles of acacia wood... You shall also make a table of acacia wood... And for the tabernacle you shall make the boards of acacia wood, standing upright... And you shall make bars of acacia wood... And you shall make for the screen five pillars of acacia wood... You shall make an altar to burn incense on; you shall make it of acacia wood..." (Exo. 25:10, 13, 23; 26:15, 26, 37; 30:1). The ark, the table for the showbread, the altar of incense, and many other items were all made from acacia wood.

Acacia wood is very solid and doesn't rot easily. Therefore, those who have the being of acacia wood are very solid. They are able to endure many attacks. We will not be solid if our personality has many problems. Brothers, are you solid? If you forget your promises easily, it shows that you are not solid. Do you rot? If you go to a movie the moment you get invited, it shows that you easily rot. Only those who are solid as acacia wood don't easily rot.

More than this, the acacia tree has long thorns, protecting it from the bites of animals. Brothers, do you have the ability to resist the world? If you move your body when you hear a pop song, it shows that you don't have the resisting ability. Whether God can use you or not depends on what kind of material you are. Acacia wood has the power to resist unhealthy environments.

Fig. 66. *Acacia Seyal* Del. var. *fistula* Schweinf. (Nach Schweinfurth.)

Hard to Knock Down

To have a being as solid as acacia wood, we must follow the Lord, lay hold of the Lord, and consecrate to the Lord. As we are made solid, we will not be knocked down by any small thing. What kinds of things can knock down? You may serve the church for half of a year and have no fruit at the end of it. You can be distressed because of this. This distress shows that you are easily knocked down. Or you may read the Bible for half a year and feel you didn't gain anything. This feeling can "knock you down." Or you may be knocked down because you don't feel your spiritual life grew. You have to realize that spiritual life doesn't grow all the time. There will be bottlenecks in the process of life's growth. Therefore, the Lord needs to arrange a special environment or give you a special word for you to break through. It is a pity that some are knocked down when they face stagnation. Because they are knocked down, they cannot break through. This simply shows that their being is not solid.

Brothers, God desires to gain material like acacia wood. Why? It is because zealousness is not enough for serving the church. The church needs someone as solid as acacia wood. Do not think it is easy to serve the Lord. Such service needs someone who is not easily beaten by difficulties.

The Bible tells us that Samuel was sad because of Saul. However, God said to him, "How long will you mourn for Saul?" (1 Sam. 16:1a). We will be upset when things happen. However, we must learn how to not be knocked down by these things.

Rejecting Depression and Frustration

Those who are like acacia wood won't be knocked down by one thing, and they also will reject becoming depressed by sufferings. Are there any sufferings? Brother, there will surely be sufferings! But those who are like acacia wood learn to have the Lord in the midst of their extreme suffering. They will learn to say, "I am joined to the Lord. I look unto His mercy to bring me through this particular experience."

Even more, those who are like acacia wood will reject their frustration when things go wrong. Someone may buy a house and then find out the house has major problems. At this time, he may cry, "Why me?" This shows that he is frustrated because of the situation. We must learn to say "no." Those who are like acacia wood should be above their situations. They should still have joy and not be limited by their environment.

Brother, how solid you are will determine your function before God. The more solid you are, the more useful you can be to the Lord. If you loosen up, you will lose your function. If you follow the Lord in a solid way, you will be very useful. The Lord can trust that you will not be knocked down by one thing, you will not be depressed by sufferings, and you will not be frustrated when things go wrong.

Being Sober with Commitment, Knowing God's Desire

The constitution of acacia wood requires that we are sober,

that we dwell in our commitment, and that God's desire is the value of our existence.

What does "sober" mean? It means you are not loose or flippant. It means you are truly joined to the Lord when you say, "I am joined to the Lord." You truly love the Lord when you say, "I love the Lord." You truly follow the Lord when you say, "I follow the Lord." This shows that you are sober.

More than this, a sober personality will cause us to insist on the good things from the Lord and the heavenly commitment. Such a personality allows us to not compromise and instead insist on the work that the Lord has measured for us. Then, we can serve the church by dwelling in our commitment. The value of our existence is based on God's desire, and God's will is our first priority.

Resisting the Things that Harm Us and the Church

Those who are like acacia wood, growing in Christ, will resist the things that can harm themselves. This will allow them to also have strong and solid leadership. They will feel ashamed when the saints touch anything that is not holy, not clean, or not related to Christ.

A congregation with an elder that does nothing will eventually play mahjong, and the elder will even play himself! A church with this kind of elder will not be spiritual, it will not produce gifted members, and it will not advance for the Lord's sake.

An illustration of an acacia tree in the wilderness. This illustration is entitled: "The outlet of Wâdy Nagb Buderah, in the Seih Sidreh."

Illustration from "Picturesque Palestine–Sinai & Egypt,"
edited by Colonel Wilson, published 1881.

Some surprising things can come in to harm the church. For example, brothers borrowing money from one another will eventually harm the church. Why? Because most of the time, the money is not properly paid back! If you manage the church well, however, the church will be solid, nothing will come in to harm the church, and no issues will be raised. Conversely, If you are not acacia wood, the church life will have all kinds of issues because you cannot stop the issues from growing and spreading.

It is impossible for nothing to happen in the church life. For example, a couple will quarrel. You cannot stop this from happening. However, if you are a solid leading brother with action, you will have the thought, "They quarreled. Let's go pray with them." Or another lovely brother may go to a movie secretly. How would you react? If you are like acacia wood, you will say, "This is such a good brother who loves the Lord. It is a pity that he went to a movie. Let's go fellowship with him and pray with him. May the Lord have mercy." In other words, as solid acacia wood, you will give Christ to others as you deal with issues.

Raising Up "The Ecology of Acacia Wood"

Those who are like acacia wood govern the church well, and the church life will be God-fearing without growing issues. This is a good ecology. The saints don't talk about money, saints dare not give a testimony about loving the world, and the church has the presence of God. If someone sins, he knows how to confess. If someone spreads a word of "death" among others, the leaders help him deal with it in front of the church. Those who are acacia wood don't compromise, and they insist on the healthy things.

Why do leading ones sometimes do nothing? It is because we are not good material. How are believers from certain local churches more promising and advancing? It is because the serving ones there are very solid. Oh, brothers, do not become rotten! We shouldn't serve the Lord in a casual way. We need to tell the Lord seriously:

> "Lord, I want to be like acacia wood. I won't be knocked down by one thing, depressed by sufferings, or frustrated when things go wrong. I want to be joined to the Lord completely. When Satan attacks and tempts me, I will insist on my commitment, God's desire will be the value of my existence, and I will live according to God's will!"

Now, you can become an uncommon servant of the Lord.

Most servants of the Lord grow to an extent and stop. Why? It is because they become common. It is because they compromised. It is because they accept who they are! Eventually, almost all servants of the Lord are ruined by becoming common. They lose their insistence in Christ. Our serving degrades, becoming unlike the serving of acacia wood. May the Lord have mercy. May we all tell the Lord, "Lord, I want to be uncommon. I want to serve in an uncommon way."

A WORD FROM THE HEART, ABOUT PERSONALITY

A man is born with two things: his being and his character. Together, these two form his personality, which is his person. If you have a good personality, you can be used by the Lord.

Most brothers are simple, nice, smart, and diligent. However, this type of person does not equal a spiritual man. A spiritual man is not a good-tempered man. When the Lord rebuked the Pharisees, he was certainly not good-tempered. How severe His word was to them! "Woe to you!" **He was not being a "good man" but a "God-man."** More than this, He didn't hold back or change what He shared; rather, He insisted on his standpoint. He would pay any price, even unto death.

Your personality will affect your life, and it determines your function in the Lord's hand. Because of this, you sometimes need to pay more attention to your personality than to your labor. This is because if your personality is wrong, it may damage you even if your labor is proper. (However, take heart! No matter how harmful your personality is, the Lord can work on you and use you as long as you love Him.)

For example, no full-timer should look down on himself or get discouraged. No full-timer should say, "I have no fruit. I am old. I cannot do much." No! A full-timer should have a personality to overcome this. If he has no fruit, he should ask, "Lord, how can I have fruit?" If he has limitations, he should ask, "How should I break through? If this way doesn't work, what is another way?"

I love to watch rivers from an airplane. Rivers are winding. The course of a river is not a straight line. A river always finds a way to go forward. This tells us that we need to learn to adjust ourselves. If a certain way doesn't work, then we should pray more and spend more time with brothers. I hope all the full-timers, young or old, respect themselves. This is a matter of personality. Then, when you respect yourself, the church you serve will be respected.

Don't get bothered. Don't be bothered by having no fruit. Don't be bothered by making mistakes. Don't be bothered by problems. Are you sad when you make the wrong decision? Yes, you are sad. Should you continue? Amen, you should continue! Will you make mistakes? Brothers, you will make mistakes as long as you continue. If you don't make mistakes, it is because you are not being presented with the chances to do the right thing. As long as you live, you need the courage to face the possibility of mistakes. Do not be afraid. Respect yourself. Respect what the Lord has committed to you. You must have a personality that is solid before the Lord. Although you have limitations, you are solid before the Lord, and your focus is on Christ when making any decision.

08 / BEING SELF-CENTERED

One of the sideways to being common is being self-centered. We can become used to a certain kind of life, a lifestyle, and a certain kind of living. All habits, however, should always be adjusted. Yet a common man, a self-centered man, cannot accept changes.

Changes always come. For example, there may be changes in the church life, changes in the way brothers lead, changes in our spiritual companions, changes in working environments, and so on. All of these changes will cause a common man to have self-pity, exposing his self-centeredness. Such a man doesn't know how to obey God's hand, how to submit to the Lord's arrangement, or how to walk according to God's authority. Therefore, it is hard for him not to be common.

Growing from "Self-centered" to "Denying the Self"

When we just begin to love the Lord, it is hard not to be self-centered. We have feelings about ourselves. We have feelings about whether we gave a good message or not. We have feelings about whether we call a good hymn or not. We have feelings about getting one person saved, not because of the person to be saved, but because it shows that we have done a good job.

Song of Songs 1:4 says, "Draw me away! We will run after you. The king has brought me into his chambers. We will be glad and rejoice in you. We will remember your love more than wine." The Shulamite was pure and absolute unto Solomon, but in the beginning, she talked a lot about herself: "the Lord attracts me and the Lord leads me." In the end, when she has matured, she denies herself. Denying our self is a high and heavenly living.

Today, it is hard to grow out of the "self." It is even harder to "deny oneself." One time, a brother was harshly rebuked in a public church meeting. The next day, however, he came to the next meeting without any issue. This shows he was able to deny himself, which is a manifestation of a big soul. His soul is so big that many other things didn't bother him. At the same time, sometimes the "denying of self" is from spiritual discernment. Take again for example the brother who was rebuked. According to his spiritual discernment, he felt that the older brother had his reason for rebuking him. He simply learned the lesson from the older brother.

Brothers, why do you so easily become common as you follow the Lord? It is because no one dares to offend you. If you were offended, you would immediately say, "I quit. I want to move to another place. I want to leave the work." Brothers, this is not a spiritual response. Watchman Nee gave a message titled, "The Response of a Believer." In it, he told us how a believer should respond. He said:

A believer should respond to God.
A believer should respond to spiritual things.
A believer should respond to loving the Lord.

Our response reveals our center. A small person is easily self-centered. A capable person is easily self-centered. A man who is good at preaching and leading is easily self-centered. In the end, these things will only harm. It is because capable people trust in their ability, good preachers trust in their preaching, and good leaders trust in their leading ability. None can tolerate it if anything goes wrong. This is being "self-centered." Blessings and manifestation do nothing but lead such ones to commonality.

Submit to the Leading Ones, Support the Servants of the Lord

The changes in the church life manifest our center, but they also help us to learn to deny ourselves. Changes to how the brothers lead also help us to learn to deny ourselves. They may change their leading every one or two years. The saints may have just gotten used to it, but then they change again. What should we do? You can only learn to deny yourself, to love the Lord, and follow the Lord under their leading. Trusting the Lord will eventually give us more riches through the leading brothers or through the servant of the Lord. We don't need to care about whether there is an administrational mistake or not. This is a small matter. There is no need to care about it. The most valuable thing is whether the spiritual riches can be released or not.

Common people will just talk about what is right or wrong. Those who deny themselves and are not self-centered won't talk about such things. **They know that their relationship with the leading brothers depends not on the brothers, but on their heavenly commitment.** "Since their commitment is from Christ, I don't want to leave these servants of the Lord."

This was my experience. At one point, my teacher began to talk about something called the divine and mystical realm. In other words, "Where are we?" The answer is we are in pursuing, in enjoyment, and in the divine mystical realm. Our pursuing is an enjoyment, and we gain Christ in the divine mystical realm. Most Christians love the Lord on the earth to pursue Christ who is in the heavens. It is hard to understand that **we already dwell in the realm of the "heavenly Christ" to gain Christ.**

At that time, I had a distinct feeling within myself, "What I have just gained makes all the other challenges worthwhile." This should also be true for you. When a servant of the Lord reveals a heavenly revelation, you will be enlightened and begin to understand spiritual things. At that time, you may have the impression, "Lord, it was all worthwhile, even if I was wronged and mistreated." The Lord is happy because you are supporting His servant.

Brothers, you may desire to serve the Lord right now. But whether the Lord can use you or not in the future depends on denying yourself when you are still young and learning to serve and follow the Lord. I hope we all can learn not to be self-centered. It doesn't mean that we follow one man. No! We don't follow any particular person. We submit to a servant of the Lord because of his spiritual ministry which reveals the divine heavenly mystery to us.

Focus on the Lord's Interests

Brothers, as the Holy Spirit moves forward in God's economy, His leading changes. However, in our self-centeredness, we usually consider whether this change suits us or not. Our problem is that too many things stumble us: the changes of the ecology of the church stumble us; the changes of the leading stumble us; the changes in our lifestyle stumble us, too.

Not only do all saints need to learn to deny themselves, but servants of the Lord must especially learn this. The Lord's servants need to realize that **a true ministry cannot be inherited.** A true minister needs to pioneer for himself, to gain people himself, to help people to love the Lord himself, to himself help people consecrate, and to himself minister to the brothers and bless the saints. A servant of the Lord, a true minister, will say:

"I have no self in any ecology or in any environment. I am not self-centered. I focus on the Lord's interests."

Brothers, allow me to repeat: if you don't grow well, it is because you are too self-centered, wondering, "Where do I go? What can I do? What burden do I have?" It is all about yourself! But if you are not self-centered, focusing instead on the Lord's interests, you will survive in even the most difficult situation.

The Transfer of Coworkers to Help Them Grow and be Broadened

The young coworkers should transfer from where they are serving every two or three years. The more places you have been to and served, the broader you will be. In appearance, you are moving all the time. In fact, you are learning all the time. You need to see more places and stay in more places so that you can grow healthily and be broadened.

Those who refuse to move will become common, since they are self-centered. All self-centered people will eventually become self-pitiful, complaining a lot because they don't know how to live under the Lord's authority.

Some people can accept the changes, while others cannot. Brothers, it is okay to refuse to accept changes as long as you can produce something better! Then, there would be no need to change. If you can't accept changes, however, and you cannot make things happen, you will be finished. Allow me to give my own example, I learned to accept all things from the Lord in the years I was under a ministry. I said "Amen" to whatever the brother told me and was willing to accept it. Why? It was because I didn't want to give any trouble to the brother's ministry. I wanted him to minister joyfully and freely according to his burden until he fulfilled his ministry.

Once he had finished his course, we also had a new way because of his course.

Brothers, we need to be honest to the Lord:

"Lord, I don't want to be self-centered. You are my center. Your desire is my center. Your will is my center."

If we have this kind of life, our existence will be high. We won't be common. We will be valuable before the Lord.

Not Being Independent

We must fight against being common. For this reason, we cannot be independent. In today's culture, it is a common thing to be independent. However, along the way of following the Lord, we need protection. Therefore, we need companions.

Dear brothers, who protects you on the way of serving and following the Lord? Who are your companions? Just like Joshua and Caleb in the Old Testament, brothers should come together to develop the Lord's testimony, fighting for the good land.

We are short of the fighting spirit, and we are short of the spirit that fights for the Lord's testimony together with companions. We need to go out together to preach the gospel among young ones or in different neighborhoods. In this way, our church life will become different. There should be no brother who is lonely. We need to get away from our small and narrow world. We all need companions. We all need protection.

09 / NOT KNOWING HOW TO BE HUMBLE

It is very difficult for most people to be humble. Humility means refusing to express yourself according to your natural talent and gift. Some people are born lowly, so it is easy to be humble. Some are born highly, and it is hard to be humble. But in principle, all people like to be exalted. For example, brothers like to preach and desire to impress people with their messages. People enjoy being manifested and respected.

I want to speak to the gifted brothers: learn to be humble.

I want to speak to the sisters who desire others to know their gentleness and capability: learn to be humble.

The Lord Looks for Servants

Brothers and sisters, learn to be humble. In Christian groups, people are always looking for high leaders. But when you come to follow the Lord, He is looking for low servants. When you give a few messages and impress people, you will easily exalt yourself. However, the Lord would say, "No. I don't want an exalted one. I want a lowly servant. My servants are for serving people." Yes, our existence is to serve the other brothers and sisters.

Humility is a hard lesson. Humble servants do not give excuses for themselves. Remember that the Lord said a servant plowing a field or tending sheep still has to gird himself and serve his master (cf. Lk 17:7–8). In other words, you are not always with people or laboring, but you must always be before the Lord in a lowly manner.

Every servant of the Lord needs to go through a long process of the Lord's work so that his heart can be stable and unwavering.

They follow the Lord whether they are busy or not.

They follow the Lord whether they are manifested or put aside.

They labor and gird themselves to serve the Lord whether they are manifestly useful or seemingly covered up.

A Servant's Flowing Out of Divinity through Humanity

Those who are common don't even think about being humble. Common men want to exhibit their talents. They excessively desire to be praised, manifested, or be in a leading position. Brothers, these are killing elements that prevent you from going on. **A good servant of the Lord always**

aims for the outflow, the fragrance, of divinity through their humanity. This is real serving. Oh, so many full-time brothers are occupied by work but do not manifest the Lord's divinity through humanity. They all want to be useful, to have a burden, to be manifested, to be praised, to be in a leading position, and to be exalted. Yet this only gives Satan an opportunity, and many therefore lose the chance to develop their ministry.

Brother, you could be tall and handsome and aggressive, but it is hard for you to be humble. Brother, you could play the piano and sing and write hymns, but it is hard for you to be humble. No one dislikes being exalted. People are born with selfish ambition. The hard lesson is that you do need to advance, but you must take care not to exalt yourself.

Brothers, **if you don't know how to be humble, you will hurt yourself when you take the lead.** Brothers, have you ever thought about being an elder? On the one hand, it is a natural process of growth. On the other hand, if you think it will be your turn to be an elder once you have stayed long enough, this is a very dangerous thought. Being an elder is a commitment, not an outcome of seniority. May the Lord have mercy on us.

10

MAKING USE OF THE LORD'S WORK & THE CONGREGATION

What does this mean, "making use of the Lord's work and the congregation"? And how does this go along with taking or finding a field to labor? This point is not about laboring. This point is about looking for opportunities to lead. Making use of the Lord's work and the congregation means that someone else has labored, yet you look for any chance to grasp their fruit for yourself. This not only makes you common but also kills you spiritually.

You could see a few saints who are together and try to gather them for a variety of things: playing basketball, singing hymns, or reading the Bible. Suddenly, you may unconsciously feel that these people belong to you. Brothers, no! Someone else had preached the gospel and labored hard to raise up these few saints. That laborer worked very hard to gain them. Suddenly, however, you, possibly a more capable one, came in and claimed them as your own. Brothers, you should not do such a thing!

We should develop a clear feeling: "I can help some love the Lord and I can help some to grow, but they are not my children." When I went back to Taiwan to give a conference in 1973, there were about 400 or 500 young people attending. However, I was clear that they were not my children. I could help them to consecrate to the Lord, but I left quickly after the conference. Why did I leave? It was because I didn't want people to follow me, and I didn't want other brothers to have any impression that I wanted to take their fruit. Today, however, people so easily grab whatever they like.

Never Building on Another's Foundation

If there are ten saints who are not the fruit of your labor, you need to be careful how you help them. The apostle Paul said, "And so I have made it my aim to preach the gospel, not where Christ was named, lest I should build on another man's foundation" (Rom. 15:20). He wanted to preach the gospel himself and to raise up churches himself for the Lord to gain His testimony. Consider this purity!

Brothers, we all must learn this principle again and again: if we desire spiritual children, we must bear them ourselves. Do not look for others' children and say, "These ten people are mine." No! Don't do it.

Some may think that a good way to build the testimony of the Lord is to take all the good saints from other Christian groups. But you have to realize that every human family has its own family tree. It goes from generation to generation. Spiritually, it is the same. Every congregation or group of saints has their family tree. If you pull out a good brother from another congregation, you actually destroy the Lord's work in that place, you hurt the rest of the believers in that congregation, and you cause other Christians to be offended and suspicious. Even if the situation of that place is not good, you have no right to take away people from there. It will produce a worse result in your serving if you do so.

Recognizing We Have "No Right"

Brothers, never make use of the Lord's work, never take away a congregation for yourself, and never try to grab people in your hand. You didn't save them, and you have no right to take them away. They belong to Christ and the church. You should let those who birthed them take care of them. More than this, do not invite all the churches to your place and never go anywhere yourself. You don't have this right.

We cannot be self-centered and ask people to support us simply because we have a burden. No, this is not for the interests of the body of Christ; it is simply making use of the Lord's work. Brothers, I hate it when people make use of the Lord's work. (I also hate it when brothers are being used by others and don't realize the meeting was actually taken away!) What kind of people are common? They are those who try to be famous and to be praised. To this end, you can "make it" by taking advantage of the labor others have done. But this is evil. In my life, I hate this the most. This type of person cannot be used by the Lord or valuable before Him. The Lord can only use those who love Him purely and know the things of life.

Brothers, we must have such virtue all our life. Do not make use of the Lord's work or a congregation. Don't think a congregation is open to you and that you have the right to take them away to make yourself stronger. No! We have a commitment from the Lord. If the congregation is looking for the Lord's testimony, we can show them the way faithfully and honestly. However, we cannot grab them into our own hands.

Laboring and Operating by the Right Principles

Don't take the easy way when serving the Lord. Yes, the work is hard. How many people must we preach to so that we can get one saved? Among all who are saved, is there one who loves the Lord? And among all those who love the Lord, is there one consecrated? Even with this as a fact, we also can never go to another group to recruit people to be in our congregation.

Remember this: even if that way would succeed, the Lord will never use you. You may gain many people, but there is no value before the Lord. We have to learn to allow people to walk the way they choose. If we are truly a servant of the Lord, He will definitely use us to raise up people. We don't need to touch the things we shouldn't touch.

Brothers, don't look for a group to lead or a group for you to shepherd. Learn to be with the church and with the saints. We need to operate by the principle of oneness in the locality. It is too easy to grab a congregation and say, "They are following me." Without knowing it, you make use of the Lord's work.

The Most Important Thing:
Preaching the Gospel

I hope the church grows purely in this way; that everyone who comes in is the fruit of our gospel preaching and grows together with us. Of course, you must allow others to join if they are led to. Don't say, "Only those saved by us can come!" This is heretical, like the Church of Christ. But please, consider the purity of the principle I am describing: do not grab any other congregation and make them yours. You must be very careful. If you do this, it may hurt the Lord's work. Even if you gain some, they will be very opinionated. No, don't do this. It will make it hard to go on. We would rather start with three or five people and go from there. When we pioneer for the Lord's testimony, don't go to any organization. We just look for the group with which we can fellowship. We shouldn't sell "local church" but look for those who we can fellowship with. If we cannot find any, we will start ourselves, step by step according to the Lord's commitment to us.

Don't try to gain a group. If some are desirous, they will join you. If the leading one of another group feels the congregation belongs to him, they will not follow you. Yet these things are not crucial. The most important thing we should do is to preach the gospel.

Brothers and sisters, **we have Christ! He is sufficient for the gospel, and He is a base for our labor.** We don't look down on any fruit. If you have a chance to speak for the Lord, speak. However, you must never have the intention of gaining people from another congregation or of grabbing people from any Christian group. This is not healthy or moral. The Holy

Spirit should be free to lead other Christians to join you, and you must be able to receive them, but this is the work of the Holy Spirit. How can you reject His work? Yet we must take care not to try to manufacture such a work.

Dear brothers, may we all learn to be humble. Do not make use of the Lord's work, and don't steal people to make them yours. No, they belong to Christ. May the Lord have mercy on us.

11 / ATTRACTED BY THE MATERIAL & RELIGIOUS WORLDS

Being self-centered makes us common. Making use of the Lord's work makes us common. Moreover, being attracted by the world makes us common. We can see in church history that after a place experienced a great revival, the world quickly came in. This world was not only material, but also religious.

The Material World:
Stealing the Time for Perfection

After great revivals, most brothers and sisters go to pursue development in the material world. I have seen this over my life. They may still love the Lord and go to church meetings. Those who have been part of a revival will find it hard to forget about the Lord, because something was sown into them. Though they love the material world, they will still go to church meetings. They only have, however, a Christian life; their Christ has "disappeared." In other words, they are still around and they still love the Lord, but you know their golden years have been used up by Satan.

On the one hand, they have been through a revival and have a basic knowledge about the divine life. When they serve, we should respect them. On the other hand, it seems impossible for them to have a strong ministry. Ministry is only formed through God's beating work, and through their engagements with the material world, they lost the most precious years to be beaten. Although they still love the Lord, it is hard for them to have their ministry.

Brothers, our God is very practical. If you cannot go through His beating work, He has no choice but to put you aside. This is the reason I often encourage brothers to serve full-time. Even when I try so hard to encourage brothers, not many serve full time. So I need to encourage more brothers! If I didn't encourage anyone, I don't believe anyone would serve full time. Who doesn't love things in the material world?

A degraded church will have some brothers and sisters who love the world but are not ashamed of it; others may even envy them. Brothers and sisters, please remember what the Bible says: that friendship with the world is enmity with God (James 4:4) and that if anyone loves the world, the love of the Father is not in them (1 John 2:15). Such saints have betrayed the Lord Jesus. They have sold their birthright.

The Religious World:
Exposing People's Impurity

Not only will the material world come in but also the religious world. The religious world is even scarier than the material. When the religious world comes in, those who are pure and desire the Lord will be challenged. Man's fallen nature, sinful flesh, and impurities are all exposed when the religious world comes in. For example, there could be arguments around whether or not the church should decorate the meeting hall and plan activities for the Christmas holiday. Or on a deeper level, those in the religious world may ask things like, "Who should we be joined with? Who should we follow?" These are impure thoughts from those in religion, as those who are in the religious world will look for their future, rather than trust in the Lord.

Dear brothers, we should not be following any brother; we follow the Lord! There are some brothers the Lord has raised up on our behalf, to give us Christ through their ministry. It is right and healthy to be related to such ones. But we should all be able to say, "Lord, if the brother who loves us, cares for us, serves us, and gathers us together is eventually taken by You, we can still be raised up by You! We desire more ministries. We do not want to be common. We are not church goers. We are not preachers. We are not just maintaining congregations. We are bearing the commitment for Your testimony!" How good such a realization is.

When the brothers who care for us are away, we should allow the togetherness of the churches to be taken care of organically. If there are some churches who cannot be together at that time, it will be okay, since the Lord is still here. When the ones who love and care for us depart, we should not manufacture being together through our own ways. No. Rather, we need to pray, "Lord, the churches are Yours. The brothers are Yours. All the brothers who love You are Yours. Lord, take care of us."

Those Who Have the Lord
Have the Most Valuable Life

Satan sends both the material and religious worlds into the church to damage us. We can consider these two worlds as representing a two-fold damage. When the material world comes in, many brothers and sisters who love the Lord are damaged by lust for money and the development of life. When the religious world comes in, many who love the Lord are damaged by their thoughts and motives becoming impure.

Oh, how severe is the damage of the material and religious worlds! These worlds cause those who have been through a great revival to lose their enjoyment of Christ, and these worlds make it difficult for the testimony in such places to go on. Through these worlds, there will be fewer and fewer of those who truly have Christ, desire Christ, follow Christ, lay hold of Christ, walk the way of the cross, and forsake all for the Lord.

People ask me, "How old are you?"
I answer, "I am eighty-some."
"Did you have a valuable life?"
"Yes, I did."
"Did you gain a lot of money?"
"Not a lot."
"How could your life have been valuable?"
"I have the Lord, the Christ. My life is most valuable!"

Brothers, you don't know how good it is to purely love the Lord and have the Lord! In the end, you have to say, "Lord, thank You for all the things in the world, but they are not my God. I desire the Lord only!" May the Lord have mercy.

12 / NOT RESPECTING MARRIAGE

Marriage is one of the most important matters for those who have and love the Lord. A common man may eventually feel that his wife is not suitable for him, and he will begin to quarrel with her, blame fate, and even argue with the Lord. Others are short of the wisdom that comes from laying hold of the Lord and then compromise because of their spouse's opposition. Still others lose their absoluteness for the Lord because they love their spouse too much and worry about them too much.

A good marriage perfects a saint who loves the Lord.
If we know how to manage our marriage well, it will help us to grow.

A marriage with "one heart" produces peace.

In other words, do not marry a Gentile. If you want to marry him or her, you must help them to first believe in the Lord. After you are married, you must cultivate your spouse's heart to love the Lord together with you. You must have Christ, the Lord, in your marriage.

A marriage with "one spirit" blesses the church.

This means that in your spirit, you care for the church, and your spouse likewise cares for the church. A marriage with "one spirit" like this will bless the church.

A marriage with "one soul" becomes the support of the church.

This means a husband and wife together are completely for the blessing of God's children. This kind of family will be a pillar in the church. If both the husband and the wife love the Lord, the family will be peaceful. Neither party will be ashamed when someone suddenly comes to your home and you don't have time to clean or to prepare a proper meal. Instead, both will be joyful and the guests will not be pressured. Honestly, through experience, the simpler a meal is, the more open everyone is.

It is a pity that many saints, even gifted ones, lose their value before the Lord because of their marriage. They become common. Brothers, perhaps you never imagined that marriage would be so critical in your life. This is indeed a huge juncture with a wide sideways path. If you cannot pass this juncture, you will lose your value before God and become a common man as much as for any other reason. Therefore, you must give your marriage to the Lord and tell the Lord,

> "Lord, if I get married,
> Make the marriage one with 'one heart,' 'one spirit,' and
> 'one soul' to bless You and Your church."

A WORD FROM THE HEART, ABOUT ENVIRONMENT & MARRIAGE

There are two things that, together, are the most important for whether you can advance in a proper way: one is your environment, the other is your marriage. We will say more about marriage below, but first we will say some things about our environment. An environment can either support you or distract you; it can either help you or harm you. Many who love the Lord in a particular locality are swallowed up by their environment when it changes.

One sister who had been through a year-long training dropped the church life when she moved to a place where she didn't know any brothers or sisters. She loved the Lord and was consecrated, so what happened? Her experience shows us that a huge challenge for any Jesus lover is a change in environment. Many saints lose their desire for the Lord in a new environment. Fortunately, in this sister's case, she truly touched the Lord and brought her husband to salvation. Now, they have a meeting in that locality that started because of her family.

Brothers and sisters, your environment is very important:

If you are with some full-time serving ones, you will pursue more.

If you are with Jesus-lovers, you will love the Lord more.

If you are in a healthy church life, you will grow more.

If you are with those who have a burden to preach the gospel, you will preach the gospel more diligently.

If you are with those who are consecrated to the Lord, you will develop well in the healthy environment.

Brothers, as you follow the Lord, pay attention to your environment. This means paying attention to the ecology of the environment. Ecology is a word that indicates the relations of living organisms to one another and to the environment they are in. This will determine church culture. A healthy ecology will produce a healthy church culture. When people come into this environment, they can not help but love the Lord and consecrate unto Him.

Second, pay careful attention to your marriage. If your marriage has problems, it will be hard for you to develop, even if you are in a good environment! One brother married a beautiful sister. However, this sister had a tendency to get jealous easily. Whenever the brother went to meetings, she would get jealous, and this caused strife in their family life. This greatly prevented the brother from developing, and shows the influence and importance of the marriage relationship.

Brothers, if you are not married, be sober about your marriage-to-be. If you are already married, try your best to manage your marriage and make it valuable. Believe me that no matter how well you "knew" your wife before you got married, you still don't really know her. You will truly know her after you get married. Likewise, sisters are the same. Wives will be surprised who their husbands truly are! Therefore, you must love your spouse and lay hold of Christ, gaining the wisdom from the Lord for how to follow Him while loving your spouse.

An environment is important, and marriage is also important.

If you have a good environment and a good marriage, you will follow the Lord much more easily.

13 OVERLY FOCUSING ON PERSONAL DEVELOPMENT

Overly focusing on personal development, both material and spiritual, will make you common. If you overly focus on your development in these areas, it will only cause problems.

An Unending Snare

Most people like to advance; this is healthy. Therefore, we should pay attention to our development. Christians, especially those who love the Lord and have a job, should be advancing and developing in their fields. If you choose to have a job, you should have a job with prospects. There is nothing wrong with a simple job, but a job with prospects will broaden your soul and help you develop as a person. However, if you are not careful, your advancement and development will become a net, a snare, that will cause you to lose your absoluteness before God.

I don't agree with poverty. In fact, poverty is the result of the curse. If man hadn't fallen in the first place, poverty would never have come to human beings. Because man fell, poverty came in. However, you know clearly that there is no end to making money. You may think, "Oh, if only I could have a car." After you get one, however, then you may think, "Oh, if only I could have a new, imported car." And then you may think, "Oh, if only I could have a new German car..." Brothers, there is no end to what you can pursue in the material world.

We shouldn't be poor. We should have a proper income. If the wife of a full-time serving brother can work and support the family, I think it is a good idea. If her work doesn't negatively affect the family or the children's education, it is good for her to work. On the one hand, their financial situation will be better. On the other hand, the wife will also have a sense of achievement. I am supportive of all these things. However, the wife should take care not to overly develop what she does into a career.

Wives, don't try to be super-women. It is not worthwhile; we don't need it. We only need a simple life. A full-time brother cannot have a wife who is too capable. If she has a career in a big company and is relocating all the time, can her full-time serving husband move with her? If he doesn't move with her, they will be separated and the marriage will not work. Yet a full-time brother must be responsible to the Lord. The Lord's arrangement for him in one locality is for the benefit of the church and for the Lord's will. His wife has no choice but to follow him. Therefore, it is not hard to see the strife that will be caused if she becomes overly focused on her personal development.

Losing God's Original Intent

Let me repeat: no one should live in poverty. However, improving your standard of living is an infinite process. The push is unceasing to get richer, to have a higher position, to be more respected, and to live a seemingly more valuable life (in the world's eyes). However, these things will steal away a brother who loves the Lord, who has talent, and who can be used for the Lord.

A servant of the Lord who is stolen away by personal development will become a common brother. Yes, such a brother is common. Though he may still love the Lord and even serve Him, he will only be a "common" serving brother, a "common" elder, or a "common" ministering brother. He may have thought he could gain both the heavens and the earth, but in the process, he lost God's original hope for him and became common.

A Word Directly to Those Who Are Rich

It is hard for us to understand that those who both love the Lord and can be used by the Lord will almost always become quite common when they develop a desire to become rich. Yet the apostle Paul said this himself: "Those who want to get rich fall into temptation and a snare and many foolish and harmful desires which plunge men into ruin and destruction" (1 Tim. 6:9).

Many of us do know, however, some brothers who are capable and who have made a lot of money. They still love the church, manage the church, and speak for the Lord. Let me speak a word directly to these brothers: be careful. You must be extremely godly, otherwise you will become a bad example for the other saints. Most saints cannot make a lot of money and still live healthily before the Lord.

Additionally, let me say another word to brothers who have made a lot of money and are still able to serve: it is easy for a brother like you to feel good about yourself. You can go to work, visit the saints, serve the church, and give messages. However, you will not realize when you cannot build up the church anymore. Why does this happen? It is because you have become common. You have everything and can do everything. Unconsciously, you have lost the poorness of spirit that causes you to fight for more blessing from the Lord.

Do you have money? Yes, you do.
Do you have a church life? Yes, you do.
Can you give messages? Yes, you can.
Can you manage the church? Yes, you can.

Brothers, be aware of "I have, I do, and I can!" "I can preach," and as a result, brothers and sisters are dead. "I can manage the church," and as a result, brothers and sisters are depressed because the leading is so "common." Let me ask you:

Where is your impact?
Where is your power?
Where is the Lord's fresh speaking?
Where is the uplifting within you?
Where is your revival?
Where is your supply to bring in the revival?

Many would answer: "Nowhere!" You have none of these things but you still feel good about yourself. You don't realize how harmful your commonness is to the saints!

The Need For Height and Depth

I know a brother who is quite capable. He has vision, and he is able to develop. This shows that he is "broad" enough, but he is lacking in height and depth. In principle, a greater height should lead to a greater breadth. This is just like a tent; the higher the center pole is, the broader the area is under the tent covering. However, this brother is not like that. He is broad and can handle everything. When brothers have problems, he can handle it. Are there a couple of quarrels? He can handle it. When there is a need in the church, he can handle it. He can also speak for the Lord. However, because of these things and without even knowing it, he feels, "I am good. I am serving the Lord. I am serving the church. I am helping the brothers and sisters." As a result, he has lost his high commitment before the Lord.

Brothers, in following the Lord, the term "the broader, the better" does not apply. Instead, it is "the higher, the better." If your message doesn't have impact and people are neither dead nor alive, it shows you don't have enough height. Actually, it may be more beneficial to the church if you don't give a message! Then saints would be forced to pray, to repent, to confess to the Lord, to seek His presence, to pursue Him desperately, and to rise up themselves.

Why is your church life not good?

It is because of the common messages. You like the messages you preach, but they are common and people are unaffected.

Brothers, don't think that you are merely serving the church, taking care of the saints, and giving messages. No! You should always ask the questions: "Is my height getting higher? Is my depth getting deeper?"

Without Reality,
the Congregation Will be Gone

There are some church meetings with tens of thousands of people. However, large gatherings are not our commitment. Our commitment is to give Christ, to enjoy Christ, and to touch the heavenly things. The size of the congregation is not important. The most important things are:

Where is Christ?
Where is the Lord Jesus?
Where is the reality of loving the Lord?

Notice I said, "where is the reality of loving the Lord?" Loving the Lord is one thing, the reality of loving the Lord is another. This reality is tested by these questions: Is Christ present? Is Christ in your life? Is Christ in your job? Is Christ in your pursuit? Is Christ in your labor? Is Christ in your service?

Brothers, do not endeavor merely for outward things. Do not become a man merely who has achievements on the earth, who serves in the church, and who gives messages in the meeting. A man like this may not bring people to life, to truth, to revelation, and to higher ground. Do you think such a man really protects the congregation? No. One day, the congregation will disappear when something negative happens.

Oh, may we all become high and not common. We are for Christ and the church. We stand for Christ and the church. We don't want to be a common brother who is capable of doing things, even of preaching, or an elder who is unable to build up the church in life and in truth. May we be careful, and may we tell the Lord:

> "Lord, I don't want to be common.
> I don't want my serving of the church to become common.
> May the saints receive a true life supply, so that they can be hopeful."

A WORD FROM THE HEART, ABOUT JOBS & CAREERS

What is the difference between a job and a career?

A job is something you do and you can leave. A career is something you must devote yourself to. A job is something you can pick up and put down. A career is something you get into and you have to become part of it.

If you consider being a civil engineer your job, you will have no problem picking it up or putting it down at the Lord's call. If you consider civil engineering your career, however, you will end up giving yourself to it and becoming occupied by it. This is just the way of the world; once you are in a career, you are sold to it, and this will make it hard for you to grow spiritually. For example, you may be a musician who joins the world-famous Cleveland Orchestra. They will tell you they are spending three months touring and traveling the world. Only a Jesus-lover would be concerned, thinking, "My environment is changed, lost, for three months! I will be separated from the church and the saints for three months!" At this point, is the Cleveland Orchestra a job or a career to you? Brothers, if you love the Lord, you may have a job, but do not let it become a career. Even if you do have a career, you should consider it as your job.

The apostle Paul had a good job, but it was never his career. He worked as a tentmaker (Acts 18:3). When he needed money, he worked a little. When he had enough, he served the church. When Timothy was with him, he worked in order to provide for Timothy, and then he came back to serve. Therefore, he said to the Ephesian elders, "Yes, you yourselves know that these hands have provided for my necessities, and for those who were with me" (20:34) Brothers, you may have a job, but guard again having a career. This is a principle. If your job becomes a career to you, you will become driven to get the top position and earn as much money as you can. Brothers, do not do this. If you do so, your love toward the Lord will suffer.

We should feel that it is precious to be without a career. Worldly people will not understand it. But you have to say, "The work I am doing is a job. I have nothing occupying me and preventing me from serving God. I just want to love Him and serve Him!" Therefore, you can put down your job at any time and even move to a new place for the Lord. There, you can find a new job. You are ready. When the Lord calls, when He leads, you can quit and move.

This is why it is good for brothers and sisters to learn a trade. If the Lord leads us to raise up His testimony in another continent, for example, we must be able to support ourselves and meet people in normal ways. This is why besides raising up churches and developing our abilities, it is good for us to learn a trade, like hairdressing, tailoring, baking, etc. On the one hand, we work for the Lord and develop ourselves. On the other hand, we learn a skill so that we can move wherever the Lord leads us. May the Lord bless us in this way.

WORDS FROM THE HEART, WORDS OF TEACHING (2)

People will make mistakes, but God's commitment never changes. We praise the Lord for this!

To serve the Lord is much more valuable than attaining a PhD or working for a laboratory. Scientific studies benefit human beings, so there is value there. However, the existence of a servant of the Lord affects others' eternity.

The Church Life

There are two lines to pay attention to in a church life: one is the practice of the Lord's table, the other is the nurturing of a fighting spirit. The Lord's table should be so touching and so very focused on Christ and treasuring the Lord. At the same time, saints should be encouraged to live lives just fighting for the Lord's interests.

The church life should be attractive, able to touch people and help them feel that they are gaining something. For this purpose, leading ones should not be afraid of paying a price. As long as we have a high ministry and a high standard for the church life, don't be concerned about fewer numbers. Of course, we want people to be saved and to come into the church life. But we must first care about our being, about who we are. This is the standing of every local church.

In the church life, young ones should blend with older ones. In turn, the older ones should protect and encourage the younger ones and let them function. In this way, a church culture can be changed to something very healthy. This kind of effort rescues a church life from a preaching culture. We should desire to bring saints into a pursuing life and a functioning life. Meetings should be opportunities for everyone to supply life. Bearing fruit ceases being a struggle; rather, fruit is simply attracted to come.

The church life is not for listening to messages. It is for the functioning of all brothers and sisters.

Speaking for the Lord

People usually develop their ministry by speaking for the Lord. Eventually, healthy speaking builds up the church.

If you have a chance to speak on the Lord's Day, you should pursue more, pay more attention to your spiritual situation, and spend more time before the Lord. You should know how the Lord is working on you and you should pay attention to developing yourself healthily. Most people who speak for the Lord are satisfied by the "amens" of others. This satisfaction prevents them from truly developing their ministry.

For some reason, North Americans are obsessed with messages on the Lord's Day. However, the Bible only tells us about the breaking of the bread on the Lord's Day. It never says anything about preaching on the Lord's Day! Why, then, do we focus on preaching? Yet, at the same time I might say, "If a brother has a ministry, it is a shame if he doesn't speak on the Lord's Day." Do you see the paradox that a preaching brother must live in?

When you speak for the Lord, the other brothers and sisters must enjoy it. In that way, they will be open to seeing something more.

Doctrine is not reality. Even if you memorize an entire outline, it is not "yours." Spiritual things need spiritual sight. Revelation is the unveiling of a picture for you to see. What you see, then, becomes a foundation for you to be lifted higher. Therefore, it is important for those who speak for the Lord not only to have revelation themselves, but also to make others see the same spiritual things.

Preaching

When you preach, it is not necessary to finish your outline. It is good enough to catch the Lord's burden and speak out that point.

The lust of preaching will harm you.

If you desire to follow the Lord, your first enemy will be preaching.

Preaching is different from speaking for the Lord. Preaching is, "It is my turn to speak." Speaking for the Lord is, "I have something to say."

Those who preach must labor among men.

If you don't labor among others, it is better not to preach.

Do not preach on the Lord's Day unless you have a ministry. Yet for those who do have a ministry, take care that your ministry does not take over the church. The church is not for the minister; the minister must be for the church. Therefore, ministers should never use a local church as their preaching place. A proper church life is not one that is dominated by one person's speaking; rather, a proper church life allows the Holy Spirit to operate freely. A minister may have a special burden, and he may even share this burden on some Lord's Days or hold a weekend-long mini-conference. However, after he has released his burden, he must allow the church to be the church.

Meetings

Regarding meetings, there is no need to look for "something new." As long as there is a life supply, it is okay if there is nothing "new" to the saints.

Even if there is nothing "new," why do you care as long as there is Christ, the presence of Christ, and the life of Christ?

Being One with Ministry

I love reading Watchman Nee's books, and I do not have any doubts concerning his work. I do not deny his books, even though I realized later on that the Lord's work has advanced since his time and some of his content does not work any more. I just leave it at that and will not attack it. My word is simply, "The time is different. Life is different. People's thoughts are different." This is my testimony, and I can testify that because of that, I am very much blessed.

When I was younger, I had a question: how should I go on spiritually? At that time, I had a feeling that it was better for me to stand with my spiritual father. We all have many teachers, but we do not have many fathers. This was Paul's testimony in 1 Corinthians. What is the difference between a teacher and a father? A teacher will leave you when he finishes his teaching. A father, however, takes care of you and observes your development. Therefore, I realized it was better to stay with my spiritual father.

At the same time, we do not follow a man. We follow the Lord. Yet the Lord has given men to share in His ministry. Therefore, we treasure and learn from those who have a ministry. Do not follow a man. Learn from a ministry. Learn to be one with the ministry and one with your spiritual father.

Being one with a ministry goes way beyond right or wrong. We are here to learn, not to be appreciated or puffed up. Does the brother ahead of you misunderstand you? So what? Do you sometimes feel that he doesn't "love" you? So what? To allow our relationships to be dictated by such things is just like the Gentiles; the Lord Himself said Gentiles and tax collectors love only those who love them (Matt. 5:46–47). This is common! To follow the Lord in an uncommon way, and to uncommonly enjoy the riches of the Lord to His body, our relationships can not be built on such shallow things. Rather, our relationships should be built on sharing the same commitment and the same vision. We can be one with one another not because we share the same interests or because one of us merely cares for the other; rather, we can go on together because we are both for the same thing.

For our growth, we need to follow an advancing ministry. We must learn to advance with the minister.

Finally, we should realize that we are together with a brother who has a ministry because of his spiritual reality, not because he understands you.

Labor Among People

How should we labor among people? Encourage everyone. Accompany everyone. Teach them how to read the Bible, how to be inspired, how to develop a truth, and how to share with others according to a verse.

If they merely come to church meetings, they will quickly become old and common. Therefore, you need to labor one-by-one. If you can labor in this way, the church will be revived after three months. If you merely preach, you will produce a congregation that is just listening to messages. Your preaching will have no effect.

Do not be content with just preaching yourself. You need to help the saints to function.

Though you may still speak, you need to also help other brothers to speak for the Lord, to share something, to testify, and to give life in the meetings. In this way, you will perfect some brothers.

Authority

Watchman Nee has a book titled, "Authority and Submission." In it, the most important word is: do not assume to be the authority.

Brothers, do not stress the matter of authority. Just live a godly life among men.

If you stress authority too much, people will leave one day when you cannot carry out your authority.

As soon as you begin to feel, "I am the authority," it means that you do not really have spiritual authority.

Authority is not for controlling others, it is for having order in the church. The church doesn't have any authority to control how people think, how people develop, how they could have a fresh burden, how they could exercise, and how they could advance. Rather than holding on to something with a strong hand, we need to realize the crucialness of every member growing up properly in the body of Christ.

A good elder with proper authority can "help" all the saints to develop. If an elder cannot help the saints develop, then his leadership has problems.

May the Lord cover me for giving my own example. It is hard for me to hear when people try to tell me about brothers' problems. My principle is that every brother is good until he manifests his own problem himself. I don't doubt anyone. If I were to begin to have doubts that someone was not pure or someone else was rebellious, then I know the saints and the churches I serve will not develop!

Development

A young man should be diligent to develop whatever he lacks.

Try your best to develop. Develop as much as you can.

You should have a fighting and advancing spirit in the church. Do not just come to meetings.

Having creative thoughts is not easy. Elders who have served for a long time will lose their creativity for how to work with the congregation. They may have the burden, but they don't know what to do. This is just like in human life, when an older mother cannot cook new dishes. She may want to, but she has forgotten how to do it. This is why it is good for a family to go to restaurants once in a while; it gives the parents new ideas for what to cook for dinner! The principle is the same spiritually: you must go out to learn; not to imitate others, but to develop.

The operation of the Spirit must go through our minds. Many brothers and sisters will say, "Don't use your mind, just turn to the Spirit!" On the one hand, this principle is precious. If, in serving the Lord, we begin from our mind, we will only encounter problems. Our source must be the Spirit. On the other hand, we should not be afraid of our minds when we are trying to develop. Creativity, innovation, and the spark of new ideas all come from our mind.

Young ones need to break through the old structure of their church lives. Do not merely keep the set-up. We need to develop.

Elders should develop the young men with them according to their portions. Do not "use" a young man. Rather than merely asking them to do things, be like a parent to them and desire them to grow and develop.

A capable brother must not only use his talent but also develop it. This is done by developing his person. The Lord is not after just using what we can do. The Lord uses us according to the constitution we have, a constitution which is built up in us over time, little by little.

Some may worry that my exhortations will create a chaotic church life. Brothers, when everyone is "out of order," then a proper order can be developed. My concern is that if everything is too orderly, it means death.

Young ones should develop the ability of coordination and the ability of taking the lead. In this, learn to trust the Lord financially. If the Lord provides, give offerings faithfully. If the Lord doesn't provide, do not be bothered.

Oh, brothers and sisters, it is so important that every member can grow properly in the body of Christ!

The Natural Life

Your talent will be the killing element of your advancement. The gift the Lord gave you will be the very thing that hinders you from following Him. Rather than merely using and being satisfied with your gift, it is better for you to develop properly and to know how to benefit the church and yourself.

When we are zealous for the Lord and offer ourselves to Him, we need to also realize that the eloquence and capability from our natural life can be very dangerous.

Your value doesn't come from your seniority. Some older ones give their opinions based on their seniority. This only hurts the church life.

It is too easy to give opinions without proper judgment for the good of the Lord's testimony. These easy opinions can be based on seniority, on our gifts, on our development, or even on our spiritual experiences that are blessings. "Opinion" is saying someone else can or can't do something; it is in the realm of what you think is right or wrong. "Counsel" is based on a proper understanding and evaluation for the consideration of building up.

Do not give opinions but counsel.

WORDS
OF A
WATCHMAN

Earlier, we said that major reasons for becoming common are related to one's being; these include elements such as: lacking the stern face facing Jerusalem, lacking the being and constitution of Acacia wood, being self-centered, not respecting marriage, or being overly focused on personal development. The other major reasons for becoming common are related to one's relationship with the Lord.

When a brother loves the Lord, the Lord becomes his focus. The Lord is the One whom the brother loves, whom he pursues, and whom he labors for. According to this brother's subjective feeling, he may indeed lay hold of Christ. However, this brother does not know that there are many crossroads on the way of following the Lord which he needs the Lord to bring him through. Of these crossroads, the most important one is whether or not this brother will unconsciously replace Christ with the things of Christ.

The Song of Songs says, "…They made me the keeper of the vineyards, but my own vineyard I have not kept…For why should I be as one who veils herself By the flocks of your companions?" (S. of S. 1:6-7). The Shulamite who says these things signifies all Jesus lovers. The insistence on "my own vineyard" and their own flocks as the Lord's companions will become a problem for all who love the Lord. It is too easy for us to determine our achievements by "my vineyard" or "my flock" while forgetting "the Lord who gave us the vineyard and the flock."

We make it almost impossible for the Lord to bless us. If He blesses us even a little, we will treat our work as the most important thing in the world. Without realizing it, we begin focusing on our manifestation among believers, and we become satisfied with our so-called "heavenly" message. We lift up ourselves, causing us to lose Christ. Even worse, the natural help from brothers and sisters around us causes us to focus on gaining the praise of man, and we become even more distant from Christ. On the whole, the result is serious; it will make us settle down easily.

Settling Down Easily

We have saints with us. We have a congregation which we may shepherd and feed. We have a congregation that listens to our messages and receives our supply. Yet without realizing it, we become common. We may feel the Lord has measured a field to us, and we may have thoughts that are objectively very good, like: "I want to be faithful to the commitment I've been given, and this is the base of my labor." However, for some reason, our pursuit becomes common.

Our prayer is not for getting close to the Lord, but for the saints we serve.

Our Bible reading is not for supply, enlightenment, or inspiration, but for preparing a message.

We begin to search for inspiration, study cross-references, and read spiritual books only for the sake of preparing a message. Perhaps this is adequate for those who have just begun to serve the Lord. However, this cannot become our long-term practice. Our long-term ministry must not come from reading for message preparation, but from our constitution.

Those who have touched this crossroad know it goes even beyond their spiritual pursuit. We also dwell among the saints, help them with their problems, and support them spiritually. However, for some reason, we find that we cannot labor according to our vision and thus work in God's economy. We become common. We become common preachers, shepherds, or elders, merely maintaining a congregation.

How pitiful this is! Even those who have served the Lord faithfully can eventually be short of the Lord Jesus Christ Himself!

Making Use of What We Have to "Elevate" Ourselves

We can make use of the little work in our hand to elevate our position among family, friends, and others we know so that we become "respectful" in man's eyes. We easily forget that the Lord Jesus was despised and rejected by men; He was a Man of sorrows and acquainted with grief (Isaiah 53:3). We seem to be faithful, but we are actually damaging the Lord's testimony without knowing it. We become a "servant of the Lord" in name, but are short of Christ Himself.

Zealous Laboring Replacing Pure Consecration

We may be very zealously caring for the saints, the church, the pioneering of God's work, the growth of the saints, and the perfecting of the brothers who labor with us. However, it is easy to learn how to do things without a pure love and consecration to Jesus. We may be very busy, but we may not spend that much time before the Lord. We may spend a lot of time preparing messages, but not much time purely enjoying the Word. The fruit of such zealousness is busyness, and we will lose the true burden for people. Our healthiness before God cannot be tested.

Those who love the Lord, who are consecrated to Him, and who are even as mature as the apostle Paul, will always echo Paul's words: "For Him I have suffered the loss of all things, yes, even spiritual things, and count them as rubbish, that I may gain Christ" (see Phil. 3:8). This is the starting point from which God can gain us.

Paul kept this testimony under all kinds of pressure,
    therefore, he was not common.
Peter kept this testimony under God's sovereignty,
    therefore, he was not common.
John kept this testimony because of his love toward the Lord,
    therefore, he was not common.

It is very easy to be common if we are not careful.

We should be wary when our conscience doesn't condemn us when we serve diligently without the Lord Himself. We give our time and energy to the Lord, yet do not seek His face, dwell in His presence, receive His love as the source of supply, or enjoy His word as our food so that we would increase in strength in His love. Instead, we merely ask Him for His strength and support in what we are doing.

The Apostle Paul never stopped his serving. He "lived in labor and serving." However, he was also "dwelling in the presence of Christ." These two must come together for us as well.

Paul labored on those who needed the gospel. The process of his labor was for those who received the gospel to grow, have revelation, and become the Lord's testimony along with the other saints. During the whole process, he also laid hold of eternal life, dwelt in the Lord, and pursued the infinite riches of the Lord. He was one with his Lord. He also had earnest labor.

How admirable this was! He was not common; and with such a balance, it was not possible for him to be common.

His love toward the Lord made him uncommon.
His faithfulness toward the Lord's revelation made him uncommon.
His strengthening from divine life made him uncommon.
His living out and flowing out of divine life made him uncommon.
His experiences of sufferings made him uncommon.
His longing to be with the brothers made him uncommon.

We may begin to labor like Paul, but we can become swallowed up by the labor. We begin to work, but we may not have Christ. We may labor but may not gain Christ. We may be faithful to the Lord's commitment but lose the Lord Himself. We become common.

No matter how old or how young we are, we need to learn:

Our time before the Lord should not be less than our time among people.
Our time preaching the gospel should not be less than our time preparing messages.

Serving is not our center. Our center is joining to the Lord and flowing out life because we are joined to Him. If we practice this from a young age, one day we may become an uncommon serving one.

Uncommon serving ones dwell in the commitment and the labor under the vision they received from the Lord. They not only work diligently, but also co-labor with God unceasingly.

Self-pity in the Process of Labor and Growing

There is a time for God's leading. There is also a time for God's work upon us. He will sometimes beat us up to the limits of our strength or even beyond our endurance. This is a big trial for many who love the Lord and faithfully serve Him.

Sometimes we feel exalted, and sometimes we have self-pity. For example, God might bless us with some increase, or the brothers are in oneness, or others praise us. We, however, forget who we are without realizing it. When God withdraws His blessings and we try so hard but bear no fruit, it is easy for us to pity ourselves instead of come to the Lord to enjoy peace in His presence.

Self-pity is a terrible seed. It will eventually make us complain, gossip, and become judgmental. If this evil seed grows and we don't deal with it by confessing and seeking God's mercy, it will damage us, the congregation, and the brothers who fellowship with us.

A life of following the Lord is a life of pursuing, a life of laboring, a life of not being understood, and a life of disappointment. However, the Lord is near. He does not change, and He never fails those who love Him. We need to learn not to pity ourselves so that we don't complain or gossip, and so that the seed of bitterness will not grow among us. We should say, "Lord, I put myself on the altar. Please work on me according to the measure I can take. If you go a little bit further, please help me to be one with You." In this way, we will be able to pass through the sufferings which the Lord measures and may become uncommon servants of the Lord.

PART 3

TURNING TO A SIDEWAY
BECAUSE OF OUR
CONDITION WITH THE LORD

14 THE THINGS OF CHRIST REPLACING CHRIST HIMSELF

In this chapter, we will talk more about the second reason a Jesus lover becomes common, which was already referenced before: his condition with the Lord.

When a brother loves the Lord, the Lord becomes his focus. The Lord is the One whom the brother loves, whom he pursues, and whom he labors for. According to this brother's subjective feeling, he may indeed lay hold of Christ. However, this brother does not know that there are many crossroads on the way of following the Lord which he needs the Lord to bring him through. Of these crossroads, the most important one is whether or not this brother will unconsciously replace Christ with the things of Christ.

For example, we may pioneer for the church, preach the gospel, help brothers to grow, etc. These are things of Christ. Should we do them? Yes, we should. Are they good? Yes, they are good. Yet they become "not good" when we focus on these things and forget about the Lord. In the end, we find ourselves doing the things of Christ, yet are far away from Christ Himself.

"My Own Vineyard"

The Song of Songs says, "...They made me the keeper of the vineyards, but my own vineyard I have not kept...For why should I be as one who veils herself By the flocks of your companions?" (S. of S. 1:6–7). The Shulamite who says these things represents all Jesus lovers. Previously, she had said "The virgins love you. Draw me away! We will run after you" (cf. vv. 3–4). At that time, she desired only the Lord and followed only the Lord. However, quickly she comes to "my own vineyard." This was her "thing of Christ."

The Song of Songs said, "...They made me the keeper of the vineyards, But my own vineyard I have not kept... For why should I be as one who veils herself By the flocks of your companions?" (Sg 1:6–7) "I" here is the Shulamite. She said previously, "The virgins love you. Draw me away! We will run after you." (cf. vv. 3–4) At that time, she only had the Lord and only followed the Lord. However, she quickly mentioned "my own vineyard." This was her thing of Christ.

It is so easy for brothers in different localities to have their own vineyard. Your faithfulness and love toward your vineyard, however, may unconsciously replace the preciousness of Christ to you. What a harm to you!

The insistence on "my own vineyard" and their own flocks as the Lord's companions will become a problem for all who love the Lord. It is too easy for us to determine our achievements by "my vineyard" or "my flock" while forgetting "the Lord who gave us the vineyard and the flock."

We love the Lord, therefore we serve the Lord.
It is not because we serve Him that we love Him.

Losing Christ because of
Spiritual Blessings and Natural Help

We make it almost impossible for the Lord to bless us. If He blesses us even a little, **we unconsciously treat our work as the most important thing in the world.** Without realizing it, we begin focusing on our manifestation among believers, and we become satisfied with our so-called "heavenly" messages. We will lift up ourselves, causing us to lose Christ.

We may also lose Christ Himself because of the natural help from brothers and sisters around us. For example, I know a brother who loves and supports us, but who also plans everything and shows us what to do. Unknowingly, our assurance and love toward Christ could be replaced by his "help." We could unconsciously begin to focus on gaining the praises of man and feeling good about our work.

Brothers, any help that comes naturally or help that is received from our natural self will cause us to lose Christ. In other words, focusing on "the things of Christ" will cause us to depart from Christ Himself, and spiritual blessings and people's natural help will do the same.

Alas!

We don't even know that we are far away from the Lord. We may feel we are successful, but we have lost Christ.

The result is serious. May the Lord have mercy on us.

Refusing Achievements Other than Christ

Brothers, if you don't want to be common, you must learn to refuse achievements other than Christ. In other words, you must learn to refuse having a so-called future, having the success of the world, or having even a spiritual future in the churches.

This is a common problem. When we pursue things in the world, we dream of having a good future in the world. When we decide to serve the Lord, we naturally want to be successful in our serving. For example, we want to raise up churches, to be an evangelist, to have a grand congregation, and so on. All Christian workers have this type of hope. However, these hopes will eventually make us common.

We must realize that when we give ourselves to the Lord, we belong to Him alone. Whether He uses us or not makes no difference. Brothers, we may have chances to be what some consider "successful," but God has the right to constrain us and say, "No, you need to rest in Me."

Brothers, when you truly follow the Lord, what you gain and possess must be Christ Himself and Christ alone. You can have nothing besides Christ. This does not only apply to full-time servants of the Lord. If the Lord has led you to have a job in the world, there is nothing wrong with it. However, you too must be careful not to have ambition in your work, letting it eventually occupy you and distract you from Christ.

I used to have a job. Yet even at that time, I knew I was for the church. I didn't have any ambition to gain promotions or pay raises. I cared only about Christ and about gaining Christ. This didn't change when I began to serve the Lord full-time; even at that time, I didn't have ambition. At one point, I served in Taiwan for a one-year training. When the training finished, I immediately went back to the United States. Why? It was because I cared for nothing but to gain Christ. Going to Taiwan was the Lord's leading with a burden. After I had fulfilled my ministry, there was no need for me to stay to gain anything else. I came back to the United States right away.

This kind of life is actually joyful. No one can hinder you from gaining Christ. People can hinder you from gaining other things. In the world, they may hinder you from gaining promotions or money. In the spiritual world, they may hinder you from preaching or from working for the Lord. However, there is no one who can tell you, "You cannot gain Christ!" You must be joyful, declaring, "I can gain Christ!" This is good enough!

Brothers, this should be your desire: "I just want to gain Christ in my life!" If you want to gain something more than Christ, it will make you common. You may say that you want to serve the Lord. He would ask you, "Why do you want to serve Me? There are so many preachers and pastors. They serve Me in so many ways. I desire only those who love Me purely! I want you to love Me, not just to serve Me." May the Lord have mercy on us.

15

EASILY SETTLING DOWN

Easily Settling Down

Replacing Christ with the things of Christ, or losing Christ because of the natural help from the brothers, will result in serious consequences: we may easily settle down, "elevate" ourselves with what we have, replace proper labor with zealous pursuing, replace our pure consecration with zealous labor, or pity ourselves in the process of laboring and growing.

The first consequence is "easily settling down." People easily settle down. However, you may not realize that it will also make you common. For example, the Lord may want you to move, but your wife refuses. You have easily settled down. Perhaps you are satisfied with your life, your job, and your companions. You have a good income and you can offer and buy a house. As a result, you settle down, and you become as common as any other man.

A Life of the Tent

We should remember that Abraham lived in tents all his life and Paul was a tentmaker. They didn't have a "stable" or "settled" life. Please understand me correctly. If the Lord provides for you, you can surely buy a house, but you should take care not to be "bound." First, do not get bound by a house far away from the church. I remember when we decided to build a meeting hall in Cleveland, I bought a house nearby within a five minute drive. Later, we built four apartments across from the meeting hall. I rented one of them. Why? I wanted brothers to find me anytime they wanted. I didn't want to simply "settle down." My life was for the Lord, my life was for the church. My life was not for my house, nor was it for a comfortable and settled living. It is hard for a settled man to serve the Lord.

Second, you may not realize how hard it is to travel after you have settled. Brothers, we are sojourners all our life. We don't know where we will end up and what the Lord will lead us to do. My point is not merely to get a house close to the meeting hall. Someone close to the meeting hall can be just as settled as someone far away. We should fight against such settling. We should be ready to move from one place to another, from one stage to another, from one city to another, and from one country to another. Why? It is because we are servants of the Lord. We can't settle down.

I am an elder of the church in Cleveland, but by the Lord's mercy, I still can't settle down. For the work, for the church, for this area, I am able to say, "Lord, You have full freedom to work on me."

A Greater Field is Waiting

Brother, you have married a good sister. However, I worry whether your wife follows you or you follow your wife. It is too easy for us to settle, and we don't realize there are greater fields for us to pioneer and bigger areas for us to grow. These two things are related. Once you are settled, it is hard for you to grow. Abraham moved a lot, sometimes with success and sometimes not. However, he was eventually very blessed. You need to be ready to tell the Lord, "Lord, if You lead me, I will go."

Christians should be different from worldly people. They desire stability. They look for a job and join a labor union, then their life is fixed and unchangeable. We should not be like them! Refuse to be common! We know that settling down is not what the Lord desires.

Brothers, do not settle down. Go out! Go to New York, to northern California, to Florida. Do not be bound by the church and live a depressing life. We should have a desire to go out for the Lord's testimony. Let's tell the Lord, "Please give us a new vision. We don't want to settle. We will go wherever You lead us!"

Such desire will lead us to seek growth. Brothers, if you want to be sent out by the Lord, you must know what you are doing. You need to be perfected. You must know the word of the Lord, how to handle the word, how to dispense life, and how to preach the gospel. Learn these things, otherwise, you cannot do anything.

Settling After Going Out

Surprisingly, you finally go out, preach the gospel, and gain a congregation for you to shepherd and receive your messages. Then, you again face unconsciously settling down. You may feel, "This is the field that the Lord measured for me. I must be faithful to this commitment. This is the base of my labor." Yes, these are all good considerations. However, without realizing it, your labor will become common and you will again face becoming common.

For example, you could be an elder. Every day, you are with the brothers and sisters around you. You watch them grow and care for them. These are all okay things. However, you can easily lose your advancing, pioneering, and fighting spirit. You become common.

The Danger of "Mine"

I have seen every capable leading brother saying, "The people in this church are mine." Not many leading ones say, "Everyone is God's child. Every brother is God's investment. Every brother is the Lord's capital. **Every brother is for the Lord's testimony.**" If you don't have this concept, you will become a preacher to maintain a congregation. As a result, you unknowingly settle down.

No, brothers, do not settle down! A tree dies when it is moved, but a man comes alive when he moves! I can testify that the heavenly life within a follower of the Lord will be more alive when he moves. If you don't move and settle down, you will unconsciously develop something called "mine"—this is "my" church, this is "my" congregation, this is "my" field, and so on. All that is "mine" will make you settle, and as long as you are settled down, your growth is finished.

Losing Closeness with the Lord

Brothers, a sign that we have settled down is that our prayer is not for drawing near to God but for the saints we serve. In other words, we begin to focus on taking care of people more than on loving the Lord. I would like to ask the elders: How many of you pray for yourselves? How many of you spend time repenting before the Lord and confessing your limitations? How many of you tell the Lord, in His presence, "Lord, I am old but I still love You"?

An elder can unconsciously feel he is above the saints. His prayer ceases being about getting close to the Lord. In the beginning, he had good prayer times, sighing by himself, "Lord, I love You. Lord, I do love You. I love You completely. Lord, I am so happy. I belong to You. I am Yours. I am so satisfied when I am Yours. Thank You. Only those who love You purely can have such enjoyment. Lord, keep me in Your presence and abiding in oneness with You." Now, his prayer is filled with all kinds of matters.

His Bible reading can be the same. His Bible reading is not for his feeding, enlightening, strengthening, or receiving visions. When he studies, the cross-references and reading of spiritual books are for inspiration to produce a good message. Perhaps this is adequate for those who have just begun to serve the Lord. However, this cannot become our long-term practice. Our long-term ministry comes from our constitution.

Brothers, it is normal for those who are beginning to speak for the Lord to be nervous. For such ones, it is okay to search for materials and to put them together as a message. This practice will even force you to be familiar with the Bible in a healthy way. But when you have served for a period of time, you cannot keep on gathering materials. You must focus on your constitution. At this time, you prepare your burden, the feeling from the Lord, and then you develop according to the feeling. You must know the saints' situation and speak according to your constitution.

Losing Ambition to Fight

When we settle down, we lose our ambition and begin to simply "maintain" the congregation. We may dwell among the saints, help them with their problems, and even support them spiritually. However, without any particular reason, we become common. We become a common preacher, shepherd, or elder, just "maintaining" the congregation.

Brothers, the most shameful thing is to "maintain." This kind of serving is one of the key ways you can know you have fallen off of the proper way of following the Lord. **The followers of the Lord don't maintain; they fight!**

Young men should be ambitious. Without ambition, it is hard to serve the Lord well. When you have ambition, the Lord will begin to perfect you. How does He perfect you? He will ask you to serve among people; sometimes He will even give you a congregation. What is He doing this for? He wants you not to be ordinary or common but active when you face the danger of settling down.

If you are careful, a congregation is one of the best perfecting tools in the Lord's hands. If you are not careful, a congregation will make you unspiritual. This is because most members of the congregation are not spiritual. Therefore, if you are not ambitious, or if you are without action, you too will become unspiritual. What does this mean? It means you know how to handle people. You know how to speak with this one and that one. You know what to say. But your words don't have Christ. You are merely ordinary and common.

In other words,
Saints are generally common, and they will unconsciously force you to be common, too.

Brothers, don't think that you have found a local church, a congregation, so that you can settle down to shepherd them. If you think in this way, you are not a promising servant of the Lord. Rise up and fight! Go pioneer. Go gain people. Go produce a flock.

What is common?
Being common is maintaining the congregation which you have.

To those who desire to be uncommon:
Go pioneer and gain people. You can only have a true burden when you gain people yourself.

If there is a need for thirty people to gather, it is okay to go and help them. However, you must realize that **these thirty people are also a "power" to drag you down. If you don't refuse to be common, fight with yourself, elevate yourself, or elevate the congregation, they will not understand when you talk about God's economy.** You will only be able to speak of how "God is love" or how "God blesses you." Why? It is because they don't actually want God; they want God's blessings.

Brothers, if you are not careful, the congregation you shepherd will make you "settle" to an extent that you will be unable to labor according to your vision or work related to God's economy. How pitiful this is! A faithful servant all his life may lose Jesus Christ in the end. He loses the Lord, and he doesn't have the Lord. He has served all his life but doesn't have the Lord in the end. How miserable this is! **The best serving results, in the end, not in having a work but in having the Lord.** If you have the Lord, you can still meet Him and say, "Lord, I failed in my work. I am sorry. But I have still gained You!"

16

"ELEVATING" OURSELVES WITH WHAT WE HAVE

When we replace Christ with the things of Christ, we not only lose Christ Himself but also eventually come to "elevating" ourselves with what we have. Without Christ Himself, what else can we do? We will make use of the little work in our hand to elevate our relationship with friends or our position among people we know so that we become, in their eyes, "respectful."

For example, you could have a congregation of two thousand people. You may not have borne them or even shepherded them. The "damage" of these two thousand to you is beyond your imagination. It is easy for you to treat them as your capital. Unconsciously, you will use these two thousand people to "elevate" your position.

Brothers, if we are not careful, we will use our little achievements to elevate ourselves. This is not a positive elevation, like an elevation of our spiritual life or pursuing. It is really an elevation of ourselves. You may say to your parents, "I got 'promoted!' I am an elder now." Your little spiritual gain became your capital, and now you feel that you have an important position.

People are complicated. It is almost impossible for the Lord to bless us. If He blesses us even a little, something unhealthy will come out. We like to "lift up" ourselves to be respectful among men. We forget that the Lord Himself was despised and rejected, a man of sorrows and acquainted with grief.

"To elevate ourselves"
Is to make ourselves seemingly faithful, but in fact, we become a servant who harms the Lord's testimony and who has no Christ without realizing it.

Brothers, we need to be cautious, telling the Lord, "Lord, have mercy on us. We need You. Lord, we ask You, as the hymn writer said, 'for a present mind intent on pleasing Thee.'"

17

REPLACING PROPER LABOR WITH ZEALOUS PURSUING

Two other consequences of replacing Christ with the things of Christ are: replacing proper laboring with zealous spiritual pursuing and replacing pure consecration with zealous labor. Let's talk about the first one.

A common man replaces proper labor with zealous pursuing. In other words, spiritual pursuit completely takes over. This may seem right to some, but in reality, this is not good.

When you love the Lord and consecrate yourself to Him, you begin to follow Him. Two things should naturally be produced: one is related to your pursuing, the other is related to your labor. "I pursue zealously" can be called "inner life." On this side, you know the indwelling anointing. Your spirit has the reality of the Triune God. When your spirit is soft, the Spirit leads you to the presence of the Lord and to proper exercises for you to practice. This is the teaching of the anointing. It is very basic for those who desire inner life.

Some important books for us to learn the secret to inner life are, "The Secret of Fellowship," by Andrew Murray, "The

Practice of the Presence of God," by Brother Lawrence (who practiced the presence of the Lord while serving as a cook), and the autobiography of Jean Guyon.

The Abstractness of Inner Life

Inner life is the best and to desire it is to desire the best thing. It is precious for anyone to desire a deeper inner life. However, there is a problem. Inner life can be very abstract. You may think you have the Lord's presence, you have God, and you are one with God. In fact, you are simply not touchable. You don't know how to contact people, and people cannot get near you because you are so "spiritual."

Sometimes, overly concentrating on inner life can cause it to become fake. We begin to ignore our health indicators. Yes, there are indicators to show whether we are spiritually healthy or not. Humanly, you can take a blood test to show your cholesterol and blood sugar levels. Humanly, there are also doctors and nurses to tell us what is wrong. Spiritually speaking, those who are truly spiritual have ways of evaluating whether you have spiritual problems or not.

When we were young Jesus lovers, we may have had a "false" sense of dwelling in the Lord. In reality, we were possibly just enjoying a feeling or an atmosphere. We may have thought we were touching inner life, but this was not true. How can you know? What is an indicator? **Inner life is always accompanied by a proper testimony.** If you are truly enjoying inner life, you must in turn have a proper testimony.

The Proving of Real Inner Life

Dear brothers, if your inner life is real, you will have the proof in your living: by the divine attributes being lived out in human virtues, by diligent labor, and by love in your soul, caring for brothers. If you can only say, "I love the Lord, I love reading the Bible, I love to pray...," it may all be "fake."

Christians must have an inner life but they cannot "just" have inner life. This is what makes inner life so interesting! We must have it; after we begin to love the Lord, we cannot go on without some kind of inner life before the Lord. Why are some Christian workers occupied by their work? They are short of inner life. Their prayer is a tool to use God. They only pray things like, "Lord, be with us and open the door for us." They use God to achieve their gospel work. They don't care about people's salvation. Even if people are saved, they don't really care about them. This is the reason why many disappear after they get baptized. Oh, how many Christians really care for people's salvation?

When I was in military school, I brought about ten people to the gospel meeting. Everything seemed fine, but there was not much inner life working in me. Without inner life, it was simply a work without much meaning.

Without inner life, you don't have a Christian life.
With only inner life, you don't have a Christian life either.

Allow me to repeat: if inner life is real, you will have the proof of divine attributes in human virtues and the proof of diligent labor.

Do you know your problem?
You don't have an inner life, so you don't know how to
follow the Lord.

Do you know your problem?
You don't have a real inner life but a fake inner life. This is
worse than having no life.

Do you know your problem?
You have done a lot to cover the fact that you are short of
inner life.

Brothers, speaking about inner life: do you know how to
sing a hymn, how to pray, how to touch the Lord, how to
dwell in the Lord's presence, and how to be one with the
Lord in your daily walking and speaking? **Do not become
a religious man. Learn to walk with the Lord. This is the
inner life.** If you are a man like this, you will preach the
gospel, you will love people, and you will love to be with the
saints. These things are a proper manifestation of real inner
life. You can tell others all you want that you read the Bible
and that you have the Lord's presence, but without the proper
manifestation, a spiritual person will know you are not healthy.
You have replaced proper labor with zealous pursuing.

What the Reality of Inner Life Produces

Yes, the inner life must have reality. When you come to
the presence of the Lord, the Bible will teach you how to
have a healthy inner life. Speaking about Martha and Mary,
we often repeat the Bible's words that Mary had chosen the

better part, the part of sitting at Jesus' feet, a part which would not be taken away from her (see Luke 10:42). However, we should understand that **Martha is the real manifestation of Mary's blessing.**

If you are Mary, you know how to sit at Jesus' feet.
You should also be a healthy Martha by serving the Lord and preparing food for Him.

What makes you common? Your practice of pretending makes you common. You hold the Bible a certain way, you walk slowly, and you say spiritual-sounding words to people when you talk with them. You may think doing these things shows that you have the Lord's presence. Actually, you are only "faking" to cover up the real situation. Brothers, your manifestation shows who you are. Sister, your problem is being short of real inner life. You think a lot about where Christ is, about where spiritual things are. You consider that Christ is here and not there, or there and not here. No, when you use your logical reasoning in such a way, you unconsciously lose the anointing of the inner life. Learn to sing a hymn to touch the Lord. Learn to read a Bible verse to come to the Lord. Practice to see things in the Lord's presence. If you can practice this, out of a healthy inner life will come a proper exhibition in labor.

This does not mean becoming "busy." Busyness can be a fruit of zealousness, rather than an exhibition of the inner life. Some know how to do many things, but they don't know how to be in the Lord's presence. Then, some learn to be in the Lord's presence, but they have doubts about His commitment when situations arise. This too affects healthy labor. Please allow me to give my own example. A particular situation came that seemed to be hopeless. However, I was clear that it was from God. I am not His counselor. I didn't know how He would solve it. Yet I never doubted His commitment.

Brothers and sisters, you may have your own preferences, and you may have made your own choices based on those preferences. However, God would say, "If you desire to have inner life, you need to learn to labor properly." Do not replace proper labor with zealous pursuing. May the Lord have mercy on us.

18 / REPLACING PURE CONSECRATION WITH ZEALOUS LABOR

Now, let's talk about the second consequence of replacing Christ with the things of Christ: if we are not careful, our pure love and consecration can be replaced by zealous labor.

A Lack of Assurance when the Lord is Distant

When we are laboring zealously, it is very normal to have doubts and worries. However, brothers, this is only a common thing. For example, a brother may worry that his musical expertise doesn't match the saints whom he serves, therefore, he thinks of taking piano lessons to elevate himself. It is useless and unnecessary to elevate oneself in this way. Think about it: if an opera singer begins to meet with the church, should this brother then take vocal lessons to elevate himself? This kind of exercise is more than unending; it is useless and unnecessary. You don't need to compare yourself with other people in this way. Your elevation should be in your constitution, in who you are.

A servant of the Lord must have the assurance: "I may not be good in various areas. However, my relationship with the Lord is good. I know His word. I am close to Him. I am sure that I can be useful in His hand. I am advancing. I am closely joined to Him." Our problem with this kind of assurance is why we begin to worry about so much as we are advancing.

We worry about even more than ourselves. We worry about the saints, the church, the pioneering of the work, the growth of the saints, the perfection of the brothers, and even more. However, we are distant from the Lord. We don't spend time with the Lord that often, we don't simply enjoy His Word, and we lose a genuine burden for people. Yet we are so busy, our healthiness before God cannot be touched by the Lord.

Previously, we had a lot of feelings toward Bible reading, but now, we just read to prepare for our messages. Previously, we enjoyed the Lord's presence in our prayer, but now, we just ask Him to do this or that. A pure relationship with the Lord has been lost without our knowing it. This is like a hymn that says:

> Once I had a fervent heart,
>   And growth in Christ did seek.
> Sadly now I love the world;
>   My walk with Him is weak.
> Day and night I was refreshed,
>   In testimony bold,
> Minding not the sufferings,
>   But now my heart is cold.
>   How was I distracted—
> The Father to ignore?

In deep grief He acted,
How can my heart ignore?

"I had the Lord, I loved the Lord, I was close to the Lord before. Now, for some reason, the Lord is far from me." This is the situation of a common serving one. One day, he realizes, "I have done everything I should, and yet the Lord is far from me."

Needing to Desire the Lord Himself

Brothers, many of you read the Bible just to prepare for your messages. You have lost the burden for people. You don't really care for man; instead, you desire to gain them. However, if you read the Gospels, you will see that the Lord didn't care how many people He could gain. Actually, many people "slipped" through His hand.

These people had seen miracles. Some were healed by the Lord, while others received special supply from the Lord. Yet the Lord for some reason allowed them to "slip away." When people came to find Him after the miracle of the five loaves and two fish, He said, "Most assuredly, I say to you, you seek Me, not because you saw the signs, but because you ate of the loaves and were filled" (John 6:26). In other words, "You only come to Me for a free meal." Then the Lord made it clear that He didn't want those who desired His works rather than Himself.

Brothers, you can only serve the Lord today because you have spent hours and hours to read the Bible and to pray and seek the Lord purely. It is a pity if you have lost your purity after beginning to serve the Lord.

Only Having the Lord from Beginning to End

Dear brothers, those who love the Lord, who are consecrated to Him, and who are even as mature as the apostle Paul, will always echo Paul's words: "For Him I have suffered the loss of all things, yes, even spiritual things, and count them as rubbish, that I may gain Christ" (see Phil. 3:8). This is the starting point from which God can gain us.

> Paul kept this testimony under all kinds of pressure,
>   therefore, he was not common.
> Peter kept this testimony under God's sovereignty,
>   therefore, he was not common.
> John kept this testimony because of his love toward the Lord,
>   therefore, he was not common.

From the beginning to the end, these brothers only had the Lord. Among these three, only Peter was somewhat limited for a period of time. Yet the Lord still brought him back and made him see God alone. All three of these brothers were uncommon to the uttermost.

The Result of "No God" in our Labor

What a pity that it is so easy for us to lose the Lord in our serving and laboring! This is a reason we become common. Without the Lord, we can prepare a message. Without the

Lord, we can preach the gospel. Without the Lord, we can visit the brothers and sisters. We can do so many things for the Lord without Him, and our conscience doesn't even rebuke us!

Brothers, this should not be so! If you do not have the Lord, even in all these things, you should have a feeling: "Lord, I have done so much, but You are far from me. I don't want to be common. I don't want to do spiritual things without Christ. I must be a man who has Christ!" When you thus insist on having Christ and walking with the Lord, your conscience will be peaceful. Otherwise, the Lord will come and ask while you are so busy working:

Where do you put Me?
How is our relationship?
Are you healthy before Me?

Brothers, do you know a sign you have become common? It is when you spend time and energy for the Lord, even asking for the Lord's strength and support, but you don't seek His face or dwell in His presence. I hope you understand one thing:

It is not you preparing a message that helps the church.
It is you having the Lord's presence that can help the church.

When you are away from the Lord, your serving will gradually become "robotic." A robot can read the Bible and give a message, but it cannot give life. Therefore, fight not to lose the Lord's face. Fight desperately to dwell in the Lord's presence.

Serving before the Lord's Face
and in His Presence

Please allow me to share my own example. I have so many meetings every year. I give so many messages every year. Do I prepare? No, I don't. Why not? It is because I pay attention to having the Lord rather than the topic on which I speak. I pay attention to enjoying the Lord rather than preparing material. Brothers, it is right to give ourselves to serve and to ask the Lord to bless us. However, in our serving, we need to pay more attention to the Lord's face and presence.

We dwell in His love, and He becomes the source of our spiritual supply.
We dwell in His Word, and He becomes our food.
We dwell in His presence, and we go from strength to strength.

Our serving is therefore not a matter of how much we do, but of how healthy is our relationship with the Lord. The longer we serve, the easier it is for our relationship with the Lord to become distant and unhealthy. I know that in some places, the brothers take turns to give messages. Sometimes, a brother would sigh, "Oh, is it my turn again?" What is this? It is called being good for nothing! There is no burden, no godliness, no soberness in the Lord's presence!

If you have a burden, speak more.
If you don't have a burden, say nothing!

How can the church advance spiritually with your attitude? Will the saints be hopeful? No, they will all be ruined by you! Do not damage God's church and God's children!

Learning from Paul

Brothers, you cannot live without the Lord Himself, the presence of the Lord, the face of the Lord, the strengthening of His love, the Word of the Lord, and the Holy Spirit. We must balance this like the apostle Paul, who never stopped serving. He "lived in labor and serving." However, he was also "dwelling in the presence of Christ."

Paul labored on those who needed the gospel. The process of his labor was for those who received the gospel to grow, have revelation, and become the Lord's testimony along with the other saints. During the whole process, he also laid hold of eternal life, dwelt in the Lord, and pursued the infinite riches of the Lord. He was one with his Lord. He also had earnest labor. More than this, even while he was laboring, he pursued desperately to lay hold of Christ, who had laid hold of him (see Phil. 3:12).

Yes,
We must learn from Paul's example. As he labored, **he didn't have one single track, but a track with two rails.** On the one hand, he labored; on the other hand, he possessed Christ.

Without Christ, our labor will sooner or later cease;
With the abundant Christ, our labor can be healthy.

The Example of Paul

Brothers, you did have the Lord in the beginning. That is why you were invited to participate in serving or to serve the Lord full-time. Later on, you must pay attention to your relationship with the Lord.

"Lord,
Just as I had loved You before,
I still love You the same today.
Just as I had read the Bible, prayed, and enjoyed Your presence
I do the same today.
Just as I had desperately pursued Your presence
I do the same today.
I labor, yet I do not depart from the Christ whom I love."

The Apostle Paul is our pattern.

He labored and pursued, and he was uncommon to the uttermost. Indeed, it was almost impossible for him to become common.

His love toward the Lord made him uncommon.
His faithfulness toward the Lord's revelation made him uncommon.
His strengthening from divine life made him uncommon.
His living out and flowing out of divine life made him uncommon.
His experiences of suffering made him uncommon.
His longing to be with the brothers made him uncommon.

Brothers, we need to learn every one of Paul's distinguishing features. Learn to enjoy God's love, to be faithful in God's revelation, to be strengthened in life, to live out and flow out life, to experience all kinds of sufferings, and to be with the brothers. In this way, we may come out of our common situation.

Labor Diligently and
Work with God

We may learn Paul's laboring aspect, but we can unconsciously be swallowed up by this labor.

We may work without Christ.
We may labor without gaining the Lord.
We may be faithful to our commitment, but lose the Lord.

Yes, we can work, labor, and be faithful to our local church. However, if we are not careful, we may lose the Lord Himself in the process. Oh, the Lord disappears! We may serve the Lord and follow the Lord, but in the end, the Lord has disappeared. How terrible this is!

No matter how old or how young we are, we need to learn:

Our time before the Lord should not be less than our time among people.

Our time preaching the gospel should not be less than our time preparing messages.

In other words, we cannot spend so much time preparing messages that we don't go to people. If you don't dwell among people, your messages will only be floating in the air. Three things should all come together for us: being in the Lord's presence, being with people, and supplying the saints. Only in this way will we truly speak for the Lord. Without any of these three, there is little value, no matter how "good" our message is.

Brothers, serving is not our center. **Our center is joining to the Lord and flowing out life because we are joined to Him.** If we practice this from a young age, one day we may become an uncommon serving one.

Uncommon serving ones dwell in the commitment and the labor under the vision they received from the Lord. They not only work diligently, but also co-labor with God unceasingly.

"Working diligently" means I work when there is a need.
"Co-laboring with God" means I do whatever God desires.

Praise the Lord!
Not only can we work diligently, but we may also co-labor with God.

A WORD FROM THE HEART, ABOUT GROWTH

Concerning the growth of Christians, there are two lines and three aspects: one line is labor and the other line is purity; the three aspects are the inner life, the exhibition in labor, and the consecration in purity. First, we have a healthy inner life. Then, out of this healthy inner life comes the proper exhibition in labor. Then, in the labor, the consecration and love for the Lord can be kept so pure, and all the labor and fruits of labor are unto Christ and Christ alone. We may say:

Out of the inner life, you labor.
Out of your labor, you keep your love and consecration to the Lord so pure.

The Foundation of Inner Life

This is a cycle in your Christian life, one that always comes back to purely loving the Lord and consecrating to Him. The inner life is the foundation. Without the inner life, your labor will have no value. If you desire your labor and following of the Lord to have value, you must have the foundation of inner life.

If you don't know life, you will not know:
The anointing,
How to be one with Christ,
What it means to be dry,

How to have the presence of the Lord,
How to receive the speaking of the Bible daily and
constantly,
Or how to have the Lord in the midst of everything
you are doing.

Brothers, if you don't know life, you may do a lot, but it is without any value. Nothing works, but life works. Therefore, you cannot ultimately have a fake inner life. The living out of life must be real. The question is not how you physically walk, how you hold your Bible, or how you may appear to be godly outwardly, but whether you have reality from the inner life.

Not Focusing on Work but Loving the Lord

This reality, mentioned above, is what can truly become others' benefit. When people are with you, they know you have Christ and they can sense the presence of the Lord. At this time, you need to be careful, as you may unconsciously concentrate on your work.

Brothers, we must never replace the Lord with our work, no matter how many years we have served. We must always tell the Lord, "Lord, I love You. I give myself to You. I only belong to You. I just want to satisfy You. If I work, it must be from Your life. If I have life, I want this life to be real."

Yes, no matter even how well we work, we should tell the Lord, "Lord, I love You. I am for You. I desire my fruit to show that my inner life is healthy."

I don't count how many people I gain.
I just testify of how much Christ I have.

I don't count how many churches I raise up.
I count the Lord's work and flowing out through me in
these years.

Loving the Lord Purely after Bearing Fruit

Brothers, we hope our bearing of fruit comes naturally
and not through our hard work. Rather than producing
something out of hard labor, we bear fruit because we have
life, and the life naturally flows out.

Speaking about life, I have noticed something special. I
have been with so many Christian groups and met so many
believers, and I have found that those who are really for the
church and for the Lord's testimony are those who know the
inner life. Some may declare they are for the church, but they
are far from life, and so their declaration has no lasting value.
What does it mean to be far from life? It means they are short
of the Lord's presence, of the anointing, and of the desire for
the Lord Himself.

Brothers, if you love the Lord and pursue Him, then you
must know the inner life and be full of fruit. After bearing
much fruit, you need to remember your pure love and
consecration to the Lord. This is a healthy cycle of growth in
the divine life.

Yes, dear brothers and sisters, when we have a pure inner

life, the proper manifestation of the inner life, and the bearing of much fruit, we must still come back to love the Lord purely.

19

HAVING SELF-PITY IN THE PROCESS OF LABOR & GROWING

The last consequence of replacing Christ with the things of Christ is to have "self-pity in the process of labor and growing." **Self-pity cannot be separated from being common.** In other words, a common man is definitely full of self-pity. "No one sees that I love the Lord so much." This is self-pity. "Lord, I love You and the elders cannot see it. Don't they know a talented man is here!?" This is self-pity. "I have preached the gospel so hard, but no one gets saved." This too is self-pity.

For many years, I have been busy traveling to many places. However, I tell myself as well as the Lord, "I directly want to bring one man to salvation each year." Do not think that this is easy. Sometimes in November I begin to get nervous, "Lord, I have not gotten one saved yet." If I am not careful, I will pity myself and hope the Lord understands that I am so "busy" traveling for Him.

Brothers, have you ever had the feeling, "Lord, why does no one realize that I have grown?" Or, "Why does no one appreciate that I enjoy You so much?" Or, "Why does no one pay attention to how I walk with You?" Or, "Why does no one praise me for paying such a big price for You?" Or even, "Why does no one say 'Amen' when I speak so well?" These are all self-pity.

In the Old Testament, Gideon used the sign of the fleece to test whether the Lord called him. The first time he set the fleece out, he asked for it to be wet and the ground around it dry. The second time, Gideon asked for the fleece to be dry, and the ground around it to be wet (cf. Judg. 6:36–40). Brother Austin-Sparks explained this in this way: when you minister, sometimes you feel dry but the saints who hear are greatly helped; other times, you feel the anointing but the saints who hear are dry. This is true. In our experience, sometimes you have the Lord's presence but the saints get nothing. Sometimes you don't have much feeling, but the saints are greatly helped. These experiences are really for us to learn not to have self-pity.

Self-pity from the Experience of God's Sovereign Work

Brothers, you may have self-pity when you experience God's sovereign work. What is our experience of God's sovereignty? It means our experience of the things and environments God measures to us, whether they are pleasant or not. For example, if God sovereignly arranged that you go from kindergarten all the way to university, you have to go through this process, whether you like it or not.

Sometimes, God disciplines us to the extent that it is hard to bear. However, we still need to bear it because this is God's working and dealing with us in His sovereignty. If you have never had this experience, it only reveals that you have never loved the Lord or understood spiritual things. If you love the Lord and understand spiritual things, you will always find God's sovereign hand upon you. Yet sometimes in the process of God's dealing with us, we don't gain Christ, but only have self-pity. "Why me?"

People like to ask, "Why me?"

We too sometimes ask, "Lord, why me?"
The Lord would answer, "Why not you?"

We sometimes say, "Lord, it is not fair."
He would say, "That's right. It is just like how you have to go through a process to finish school; spiritually, there is no difference. I don't want you to have self-pity. I want you to learn to be one with Me and to proclaim that you are one with Me."

"Of Him, through Him, to Him are All Things"

Because of an administrational mistake, I had to go through military service in Taiwan twice. I remember the second time I went. As I was riding the train, I was singing the hymn: "The way of the Cross means sacrifice." My train stopped at a particular station, and just on the other side happened to be the train my former comrades were taking to go home from our basic training! They had just been discharged and were wearing everyday clothes. The one beside the window saw me. He yelled, "Titus, you are going again!" At that moment, I did pity myself. Up until that moment, I had not had any self-pity. But I said, "Lord, You may treat me badly, but You cannot humiliate me." Then I closed my hymnal and put away my Bible. What was this? Self-pity.

I did not read my Bible at all after that. I didn't sing hymns anymore. I decided to stay angry with the Lord. Yet after two weeks, I couldn't stand it anymore. I thought it was better to surrender to Him. I couldn't overcome the Lord. So one afternoon, I knelt down in the corner of a field and prayed, "Lord, I am sorry. I lied to You. I had said 'I love You.' Actually, Lord, I don't love You that much. You gave me a little difficulty, and I could not stand it." I repented to the Lord. His anointing recovered me immediately.

Either that night or the next day, my company commander came with a letter in his hand that proclaimed, "Who-so-ever has been through military training doesn't need to stay anymore. You are discharged." This meant me! Praise the Lord. The Lord is indeed humorous! I went home joyfully.

It so happened that, at that time, there was a three-month training in the church. In those three months, the Lord spoke to me every morning, afternoon, and evening. I didn't understand His speaking at that time. However, after ten years, fifteen years, His speaking became my vision and the foundation for me to follow Him and serve Him.

Brothers, you must realize that God's sovereign hand is ready for those who love Him and who consecrate to Him. It is just like a hymn that says:

"Father, I know that all my life is portioned out for me."

The Lord has arranged everything. He knows everything. He will not disappoint those who love Him. Paul said, "Or who has first given to Him and it shall be repaid to him? For of Him and through Him and to Him are all things" (Rom 11:35–36a). Yet in the process of these "all things," we may have self-pity.

The Goal of God's Sovereign Hand

It is so easy for us to pity ourselves. We may think: "Why do I live like this? Why is my house like this? Why do I only make this much money?" Or, "Why do I only lead hymns? Why can't I speak the messages?" We have a lot of self-pity about many things. **Self-pity will make you lose your purity in Christ.** Brothers and sisters, when we go through the work of God's sovereignty, we must learn to say:

"Lord, I give myself to You!
I put myself on the altar.
Please work on me according to the measure I can take.
If You must go a little further, please help me to be one with You."

Brothers, when we can pray this, the Lord will bring you through things to the point that you understand:

You have no one besides Christ.

You have no other spiritual achievement besides Christ.
You have no serving outside of Christ.

After you pass through God's sovereign hand, it will generate high spiritual value. This value only comes, however, from God's dealing with you in His authority. There is no other way. Many times, the things from God's hand won't go away, but God is there!

God's Way has It's Time

As we labor and grow, we must understand that there is a time for God's blessing, a time for God's leading, and a time for God's work upon us. This is a huge trial for many saints who love the Lord and serve Him faithfully. In other words,

There is a time we feel everything is smooth.
There is a time we feel there is no way to go.
There is a time we feel the Lord's presence is obvious.
There also is a time the Lord withdraws His presence for us to learn to seek Him only.

In the process, sometimes we are high, and sometimes we have self-pity. This is normal, but common. We can experience God's blessings: our numbers increase, the brothers are in oneness, and the praises come. As a result, we elevate ourselves and forget who we are. When God withdraws His blessings and we try so hard but produce nothing, it is so easy for us to pity ourselves and depart from the Lord Himself, from peace in His presence, and from the stableness of His leading.

Self-Pity: A Terrible Seed

Watchman Nee adapted a hymn that says:

Every moment, every member,
  Girded, waiting Thy command;
Underneath the yoke to labor
  Or be laid aside as planned.

It is hard for us to pass these crossroads. We feel the value before the Lord when He uses us; yet when God withdraws His blessings, we feel we are not useful and lose the meaning of living. Self-pity is a terrible seed. It will eventually make us complain, gossip, and become judgmental. If this evil seed grows and we don't deal with it, repent, and seek God's mercy, it will damage us, the congregation, and the brothers who fellowship with us.

Brothers, when the Lord does not use us, we can have two reactions: the first is we pray more, seek the Lord more, live in His presence more, and lift up our eyes to Him more. The other is we have self-pity and gossip. **Much gossip in the church life actually comes from self-pity.**

The Lord is Near:
Receive Everything from Him

In the process of labor and growing, we will have self-pity if we are not careful.

Brother Nee learned to fight against self-pity. When he saw

M. E. Barber's hymns, he also wrote a few hymns and showed them to her. She simply tore them into pieces and said, "It is useless for a young man to write hymns." Another time, M. E. Barber asked Leland Wang to baptize some people. Watchman Nee asked, "Why don't you let me do it?" She answered, "He preached the gospel to them, so he should baptize them." The next time, Brother Nee got some people saved, but Miss Barber still asked Leland Wang to baptize them. Brother Nee asked again, "I got these people saved. Why are you asking him to baptize them?" She only said, "I like it this way." Brothers, how would you respond? When Watchman Nee faced these kinds of situations, he learned to take them from the Lord. In doing this, he protected himself against self-pity.

Brothers and sisters, we will definitely have difficulties on the way of following the Lord. Do we realize that any difficulty is good for us? If you don't submit and accept it but resist it, eventually you will have a lot of complaints. Be careful! Complaints will harm you, the brothers and sisters, and the church.

Our life of following the Lord is a life of pursuing, a life of labor, a life of not being understood, and a life of disappointment. However, the Lord is near. He doesn't change. Learn to take everything from the Lord, so that you would not have self-pity and complain, gossip, or have a root of bitterness.

Do not get Beaten by the Environment but Love the Lord Faithfully

Brothers, the environment from the Lord's hand can have

two results: one is we overcome it and are revived; the other is we are beaten by the environment. When people are beaten by their environments, they become very common. If a brother cannot preach, take the lead, or find a place to minister, he may allow the environment to beat him. He will thus complain, and this complaining makes him common.

Brothers, if I can be honest with you, it is impossible for a servant of the Lord to have nothing to complain about as he follows the Lord. Do you think the apostle Paul had nothing to complain about? Do you think the apostle Peter was always appreciated? However, a true servant of the Lord doesn't complain about such things. He learns to take all things from the Lord, saying, "Lord, thank You for Your arrangement. I just want to love You and serve You faithfully." In this way, such a servant will be an uncommon man.

Yes, we can overcome what the Lord measures to us.
We may become an uncommon servant of the Lord.

Let's pray to the Lord: "Lord, we praise Your wisdom and Your power. You are our Lord. Thank You; You care for our person, for our pursuing, and for our perfection."

20 / A FINAL WARNING

Dear brothers, if you don't want to be common, you need to refuse all the points we mentioned before. In the end, there are still three more points which cause us to go astray and become common:

- Becoming obsessed by spiritual things, rather than Christ, especially preaching or being manifested in leadership.
- Our outward operation develops more than inner life.
- The focus given to us by the Lord is deviated or distracted by a good living, the world, a healthy fresh burden and commitment, success in life, or success in serving the Lord.

Obsessed by Spiritual Things

When I was a young man, I knew a brother who loved the Bible. He read the Bible, marked up the Bible, and came up with what he felt was a good message. The message was about how the Chinese are "God's chosen race." Brothers, you may smile or even laugh at this story, but it really happened! I believe it also provides a warning to us. We can be readers of the Bible, marking it up, and getting involved with Greek words, Latin words, etc. But in the process, we can become obsessed by this spiritual thing called "studying the Bible," and we may lose Christ Himself.

This example has to do with Bible reading. But there are actually many spiritual things we can be caught by and that can be obsessed over, losing Christ in the process. For example, many brothers are easily obsessed with preaching. They love to preach whenever they have a chance. Yet they don't have any feeling when the saints do not respond. They enjoy preaching and indulge in it, as if they are addicted to it. Brothers, I have said this before, but I remind you again that preaching is the biggest enemy in your life. There is nothing wrong with preaching; and there is a joy in releasing a burden and in speaking for the Lord. But the thought "I must preach" is wrong.

You may want to argue, but I would ask, "Why must you preach on Sunday morning?" A good meeting could be like what the apostle Paul described, where everyone "has" something (see 1 Cor. 14:26). You may ask, "But what about those who have a burden?" Can you be creative? Those who have a particular burden can use other times to fulfill their ministry. For example, you may have a burden to help saints to read the Bible. You could spend two hours on Saturday mornings to teach the saints who have the desire to read. Or you might have a burden to help the saints to enjoy hymns. You could spend two hours on weekday evenings to teach the saints how to sing or even compose new hymns. In this way, the church life would be so colorful! Why must you preach on Sunday mornings? Don't get yourself caught with preaching. Instead, get yourself caught with caring.

If you have a burden for newly saved ones or for brothers who have fallen away, then you have a responsibility to visit them or to go to their homes to have the Lord's table. This is the right way to labor. When you go visiting, do not give people a feeling that you want them to go to meetings. You should say, "Brothers, how are you? Here, I've brought some oranges for you."

Do you know how to restore brothers? You should bestow honor to them.

You know they are weak; this is why they need restoring. But remember that Paul said that there are members of the body which we think to be less honorable, and on these ones we bestow greater honor (1 Cor. 12:23).

Your visit should be "easy." Do not preach at them. Just care for them. You should have a feeling, "I love the brothers. I love the saints. I love to be with them." If you offend a brother so that he doesn't come to meetings, you should invite him out for dinner and apologize to him, so that you can restore him. Do not argue about who offended whom or about who was right and who was wrong. Brothers, these things are not important. The most important thing is that the other brother can love the Lord, he can love the saints, and he can come back to the church life.

I don't look down on preaching. If there is no speaking in life in the church life, the saints will be short of nourishment. However, if you think only preaching is effective, then you are expecting wonders. In reality, it takes a long time, a lot of fellowship, and a lot of labor for a small door to be opened by the saints to have the reality of the messages. This "long time" is the way of serving the Lord.

Outward Operation Develops More than Inner Life

It is very normal for the outward operation of most people to develop more than their inner life. For example, ministering brothers usually speak something beyond where they are. Yet this is actually the only way to grow! If we only speak what we understand, we will not develop. At the same time, they could have two reactions to their own speaking: the first is that they will simply give more messages to gain more inspiration. This way is not good. The second is that they would seek to really understand what they were talking about. This requires them to know the inner life and say, "Lord, I am not enough. Perfect me!"

Brothers, **if you know how to be perfected by older saints, you will be so blessed.** You may be smart, you may have a lot of experiences, and you may read the Bible many times. But more than all these things, you must learn to have a spirit of learning. Without this spirit, you cannot get much help. Look, the brothers all love the Lord. No one doesn't love the Lord. The problem is there are so many who have the spirit of doing, but who has the spirit of learning? After you have loved the Lord, you do need to develop in your operation, but you also need a spirit of learning. You need to tell yourself, "I must learn. I must learn as much as possible."

Brothers, by the Lord's mercy, this is my own testimony. I was one hundred percent a learner of my teacher. I never followed a man, but I followed a ministry. When following a ministry, it goes way beyond right or wrong. I knew I could gain precious things from the Lord by following the ministry, and for that, I am joyful to this day.

I do know a secret:

> I insist on my commitment. and I try to develop the things that God has committed to us through the brothers ahead of us. I treasure these things. And I want to continue in the things I treasure.

When you follow the Lord, you ought to be free to enjoy any riches of the Lord to His body. But in that enjoyment, it is also a blessing to have someone who can render you discipline. Strong discipline and restriction can only come when you have a commitment. Otherwise, you will only run away from such discipline, and it will not have its perfect work. We all like to do the things we will. When God created man, He did give man a free will, saying, "Of every tree of the garden you may freely eat" (Gen 2:16). But at the same time, He also gave the man a restriction: "But of the tree of the knowledge of good and evil you shall not eat" (v. 17a). In like manner, you can enjoy all the riches the Lord has prepared for His body, but you also need to be constrained. If you don't accept any constraint, it is not a blessing.

Brothers and sisters, get protection from older brothers. I encourage you all to have an older brother who you can fellowship with, who you can listen to, and who can offer you advice and encouragement. This will help you to be perfected and prevent you from developing your outward operation too far beyond your inner life.

Deviated from the Lord's Focus

Lastly, we may deviate from the focus given to us by the Lord, a focus which is the Lord Himself, by what everyone else wants. This changes with different seasons of our lives. For example, we could be distracted by **a good living,** by the world (including the religious world), by success in life, or by success in serving.

Yes, we should be careful whenever it comes to desiring a good living. I do not mean we need to take a vow of poverty, but we do need to care for what our heart is set on. For example, because of God's mercy, I designed a house in a certain province of China that has eight bedrooms. There is a balcony on the second floor with a great view. This may seem like I was trapped by a desire for a good living. However, let me tell you my desire: I would like to invite fifteen brothers at a time to spend a week or two together with me. After each group leaves, I would invite another group. In this way, I don't need to travel (which is becoming harder for me to do), but I can still help brothers to touch the Lord, to read the Bible, to learn to use study tools, to develop the truth, and to write. My motive is good, and my conscience is at peace. A servant of the Lord doesn't need a house like this, but the Lord knows that

I have the need because I am old. The Lord has had mercy on me to prevent me from departing from Him.

A good living may cause us to go astray. Likewise, **the world** (including the religious world) can do the same. In the world, we can be distracted by **success in life.** For example, when you reach a certain age, usually an older age, you will start to pay attention to how your school classmates have done: among them, is there a president, a cabinet member, a CEO, a famous author, and so on? You need to be warned to come back to the Lord. You will hear the Lord say:

> *"Do you think it is a waste to give all to Me? No! Have you found out that I have repaid you more than what you ever gave up? The meaning of your living is so real. The focus of your life is so high. My provision is the best for you. I don't owe you anything. All that you have is from Me."*

Brothers, do you know God like this? Can you tell Him, "Oh God, You don't owe me a thing. Everything I have is from You. I know You are the center of my life. I want to live this kind of life. It is the most precious living anyone could have!"

Once, I met with some of my former classmates in Washington D. C. Many of them had worked in the Library of Congress and were about to retire. I was different. Though I was the same age as them, my life was about to "begin"! At that time, I truly felt the Lord didn't owe me anything. How thankful I was to Him! I remembered when I was young, giving myself to the Lord in tears, and then having a hard time as I followed a brother's ministry. (I am still thankful for that brother. I love that brother. No matter how he treated me, his ministry was the best for me. I learned how to get help from his ministry.) Yet I could testify that it was worth it. And today, I still testify that the Lord doesn't owe me a thing!

Along the way of following the Lord, we may become occupied with the religious world. In this world, we can be distracted by **a fresh burden or commitment** or by **success in serving.** We may just focus on our burden in the church life. The burden may be healthy, but the problem is that we so easily forget about the Lord when we have that burden! We remember nothing but our burden. No, Christ must be the first priority, and the Lord must be our Lord even though we have a healthy burden.

Success in life or in serving shouldn't become a hindrance. We don't need success in life or in serving. We are just simple brothers who serve the brothers. However,

We should not be common!

We should be simple in our self-evaluation, but fighting to be uncommon! Who are common? If you focus on your operation and people merely think you are doing well, it shows that you are common. Being occupied by spiritual things shows that you are common. Being a "good leading one" shows that you are common. Being a "good preacher" and speaking every Lord's Day shows that you are common. There are many people good at preaching in the world. There are so many preachers today. The question is: Who has true value before God? Of course, everyone has their value before God. This is correct, but it is also common. We must learn to say:

> "I refuse to be common!
> I refuse to be a 'preacher.'
> I don't care how good my message is. I only care about how much Christ I have, how much I love Christ, and how much Christ flows out of me. I only care to be with brothers and to bring them to Christ!"

> Brothers, if you desire to be an elder as a status, you are common.
> If you desire to be a manifested coworker, you too are common!

The Lord has given us a focus. We may lose this focus because of a good living, the world, a healthy burden, or success in life or in serving. When this focus deviates, we become common. The things we "have" only serve to make us common!

Brothers, is your goal to be successful? No, change your goal! Instead of aiming for success, aim to be uncommon! We should serve the church according to the Lord. No one should desire to be a leading one leading and carrying out the work in a particular area. We are just brothers loving brothers. Can we say, "I only want Christ, to be purely for Christ, and to gain more of Christ!" If operation comes, so be it. But your focus is still Christ. Brothers, can we pray, "Lord, give us this kind of purity, a purity just to love You!"

We are uncommon when we have only the Lord.
We want to love the Lord in this way to satisfy Him.

WORDS FROM THE HEART, WORDS OF TEACHING (3)

When we serve, we should not promote being "in the flow."

Everyone has the right to love the Lord and to follow the Lord according to His leading. We just need to be regulated by truth.

If you have someone you can trust and listen to, how blessed you are!

Going through a "military-like training" will help you to use your time properly, and it enlarges your capacity to pass through difficulties in the future.

Working for the Lord

The principle of working for the Lord is diligence.

Helping the saints to truly have the Lord will bring in real change among them.

Do not pursue a strong move of the Lord, like a revival. Just labor with Him diligently. A strong move from the Lord, that is, a strong work of the Holy Spirit, is usually generated by apostles, not from our labor.

For this reason, do not pursue a great revival, but pursue

"a fruit." If one day the Lord leads you to another state or city, you need to know how to preach the gospel and how to help one person to read the Bible. This becomes your spiritual survival. Through two or three people you contact, you may even raise up a church. If you don't have this ability, you can only wait for the Lord's blessing, and you will be unable to develop the Lord's blessing.

Young People's Operation

First, I will say this: Do not obsess over outward operation.

Second, young people should operate with the elders in the church life, not to replace them, but to support and strengthen them.

Do not promote a movement. Movements don't work. In the end, being caught up in a movement will only harm your ministry and your name. It will not help the church.

When you consider the advancement of the church, young people need to see the resources of the elders and many homes. Homes are the most crucial element of operating. You need homes that are open to whatever the Lord has burdened you with. What does "open" mean? Practically, it means they are available to stand with you twenty-four hours a week, and their refrigerator is always available. These homes are your base. To such homes you can bring new ones, and there, you can love new ones, care for them, and provide both physical and spiritual food. Then, you should freely and creatively do many kinds of activities. For example, you should have a musical gathering to bring all the new ones together. At this time, you can sing songs that you like, not songs that older saints want you to sing.

Homes are your base. Then anywhere else can be a field to labor in. Nursing homes, university campuses, neighborhoods, and even the saints are fields. Then, you can have a burden. For example, you can have a burden to preach the gospel! Then, why are you visiting a saints' home? It is for a home for the gospel! Why are you laboring to revive or restore a saint? It is for more of the gospel! Your burden will direct all of your labor.

Young ones should learn to go out and pioneer. Get away from your comfort zone.

Don't plan too much and then lose all of your burden.

For spiritual work, "I do it" is not important. It's about what kind of person is doing the laboring. Don't forget that it is still a spiritual thing. But at the same time, it is easy to be caught by "feeling" something should be done, yet lacking action. Everything that a saint "feels" should be done, encourage them to do it! Encourage all the saints to have an attitude of, "I will do it!"

You must use homes. If you can use homes, whatever you do will work, no matter what your burden is. If you fail to use homes, you will not be able to carry out your burden. Use the saints' homes, and your labor will not pressure people.

Labor according to God's leading. When you finally do

something, remember two principles: First, in everything, have corporate prayer with the saints. For example, if you have new contacts, everyone should pray together for them. Second, do not depart from stable homes. When you have the support of open homes, it is much easier to gain fruit.

Do Not Fear Offenses

Whenever the Lord moves, there will be a mixed multitude.

We should not want to offend people purposely. However, do not fear "offending" others. Sometimes, especially because of the mixed multitude, people have to be offended because you are not here to merely have a religious life.

An offensive man is sometimes useful to the Lord because he exposes others. If telling the truth offends people, do not be bothered. No one can be offended unless there is something in him to be offended. This is not a small matter. In a setting where a local church has no "offenses," the Lord may eventually remove their local testimony because there is no reality of what the Lord desires.

Testimony and Ground

Without the ground of "locality," it is impossible to have the testimony of oneness.

Those who speak or minister must understand that this is our commitment: Not just "oneness" or even "a testimony of oneness," but "a testimony of oneness in locality." When you invite brothers to minister, you must consider whether that invitation will profit the saints' advancement with our commitment. We can and should have fellowship with all Jesus lovers. Fellowship is one thing. But it is another thing to publicly speak, because messages "lead" the church. We do have a vision and commitment from the Lord. We cannot invite just anyone to have a conference or give messages. Brothers, why are we here? We are here to fight for the testimony of oneness in our locality.

For this testimony, we need the ground of locality. Most people look down on this ground. This is not wise. We don't realize how crucial the land is. Without land, how can we build a house? God desires the building of a dwelling place, a spiritual house. For this purpose, He has given every church a local land--the city it is in. But for some reason, we ignore this! Spiritually, we should realize that the locality means nothing to God. What matters is the spiritual house built upon that land. However, without the ground of locality, the church will just divide and divide and divide. There will be no chance to have a proper building. By holding the view of the oneness of believers on the local ground, you will understand that the body of Christ cannot be divided. Again, I say that we have this commitment from the Lord: the testimony of the oneness of the church in our locality. We are for this commitment.

The "local church" is not determined by taking a name. Nor is it determined by the size of a congregation. If we see the oneness of the church in our locality, we will realize that even if our congregation is smaller, we include the larger congregation in our "oneness" anyways! A larger congregation, without the ground of oneness in locality, has three possibilities for their future: first, becoming an organization, that is, institutionalized; second, fading away when the leader dies; or third, endlessly dividing into smaller groups.

What, then, is a healthy local church? First, a healthy local church is standing on the ground of locality. While standing in this way, you must then consider: Is Christ your center? Are you inclusive? Are you biblical? That is, do you practice according to the revelation of the Bible? Finally, do you make an effort to be in fellowship with other local churches in the body of Christ? If these things are not present, your "local ground" has in fact become a local denomination.

Leaders, Vision, and Leading

People are always looking for a leader they can follow.

A particular group's rise is usually due to the charisma of their leader.

There are two ways to raise up a church: one is based on strong leadership; the other is based on having a leader with vision. If leaders do not have the same vision, or if speakers are invited who do not have the same vision, the church will end up going in different directions, because different visions will produce messages that have different leading.

Guarding Ourselves with Godliness

Being thankful is a huge matter.

Do not criticize the serving ones. The spirit of criticism will harm both the capacity and the impact of those who serve.

Do not attack those who are fruitful and who raise up pillars.

Do not listen to gossip. Those who do are like flies attracted to a manure pit.

If people gossip to you, just tell them, "I am not interested. Let's pray."

What will guard you?

First, preach the gospel, have the Lord in the church life, and flow out a godly life.

Second, do not listen to ungodly words. Just pay attention to the words of life which build you up.

Leaders: Avoid Having a "Pocket Church"

You need a field, but you cannot be occupied by the field. Having a field is for you to have Christ, to grow Christ, and to develop in Christ. If you have a field but you only have this field, there is a problem. This will result in a so-called "pocket church," that is, a church in someone's pocket. This leader will treat his church as his child. No one can touch it. No one can give advice. No one can fellowship with it. If anyone outside talks to a brother in the church, the leading one becomes nervous. He is completely occupied by his field.

How can a leader avoid having a "pocket church"?

You must first realize that the local churches are the local testimonies of Christ and of the body of Christ. Therefore, the saints belong to Christ, not to you. Then, you must try to bring the saints into fellowship with other local churches.

It is easy to unconsciously replace the Lord Himself with the success of your work. No! No matter how much you do and no matter how many fields you have, you must take care not to replace the Lord with your field.

The work belongs to Christ. The churches belong to Christ. All the believers belong to Christ. If a leading one thinks, "Oh, I developed it," he is spiritually finished.

If you merely guard your church to the end, saying "This is mine," it will actually harm the Lord's testimony. We should instead tell the Lord, "Lord, I am here for You. Therefore, I am here for You to send me to another city. I need fresh exercise. I need new development for Your testimony."

May the Lord have mercy on us.

CHINESE EDITOR'S EPILOGUE

Praise the Lord for His servant's warning and teaching. Today, we still have a chance to truly face ourselves and to be exposed and enlightened so that we may have a true repentance before the Lord.

This is not a "happy" book.

This book describes twenty points or two chapters of the "side ways" we face. Every one of these ways leads us away from the Lord's way, makes us lose our healthy condition before the Lord, and causes us to lose not only our focus on Christ but also our highest value before God. We should consider every point before the Lord. If we are enlightened, we will be in tears: "Lord, I am so far from Your hope for me! Lord, have mercy on me. This is indeed my situation!"

The apostle Paul wrote:

"But all things that are exposed are made manifest by the light, for whatever makes manifest is light. Therefore He says:
'Awake, you who sleep,
Arise from the dead,
And Christ will give you light.'"
(Eph. 5:13-14)

Yes, today is the day to be enlightened! Today is the day to wake up! The Lord is sounding in the night watch: "My children, awake! Do not be satisfied with today's life. Do not stop advancing. Rise up and follow Me! Have Me only and focus on Me only so that you will not be common!"

A Sweet Savor

THE MINISTRIES OF TITUS CHU AND HIS CO-WORKERS

The website www.asweetsavor.org is committed to presenting and preserving the ministries of Titus Chu and his co-workers. The heart of these ministries is to present Christ and to encourage every believer's subjective experiences of Christ, to foster the growth of their spiritual life, and to fill them with visions and revelations. In line with the heart of these ministries, this website seeks to challenge all believers and seekers of God to press on towards perfection for the strengthening of the local churches.

The website contains:
- Message Archives
- Bible School
- Books
- Songs & Hymns
- Articles
- Fellowship Journal

BOOKS BY TITUS CHU

Books are available on Amazon.com and asweetsavor.org.

On Spiritual Growth
* Born Again: Our New Life in Christ
* Come to the Presence of the Lord
* Two Manners of Life
* Visions and Revelations (Vol. 1 & 2)

On Old Testament
* A Sketch of Genesis
* Threads Through Exodus
* The Song of Songs: A Divine Romance
* The Divine Experiences in Psalms (Vol. 1, 2, & 3)

On Biblical Figures
* David: After God's Heart
* Elijah and Elisha: Living for God's Testimony
* Moses: A Man for God's Testimony
* Ruth: Growth Unto Maturity

Bible Studies
* A Study of Acts (Vol. 1, 2, & 3)
* Romans: "The Gospel of God" (Vol. 1, 2, & 3)
* Philippians: "That I May Gain Christ"

Made in the USA
Middletown, DE
12 June 2022

66915765R00135